What is *Abstraction*?

Andrew Benjamin

What is *Abstraction*?

A.D. ACADEMY EDITIONS

Acknowledgements

I would like to acknowledge the help and advice I received from a number of colleagues and friends during the preparation of this book. In particular I would like to thank Stan Allen, Shirley Kaneda, Michael Kelly, Greg Lynn, David Moos and Saul Ostrow. I would also like to thank Rachel Bean, Andrea Bettella, Sonia Brooks-Fisher and Nicola Kearton for their exemplary editorial and design skills. My thanks are also due to the artists Lydia Dona, Helmut Dorner, Stephen Ellis, Shirley Kaneda, Jonathan Lasker, Fabian Marcaccio and David Reed for their work included in this publication and the following galleries for kindly allowing me to reproduce the work of the aforementioned artists: André Emmerich Gallery (New York), Bravin Post Lee (New York), Brooke Alexander (New York), Feigen Inc (Chicago), Galerie Bärbel Grässlin, Galerie Rolf Ricke (Cologne), Jack Shainman Gallery (New York), LA Louver (Los Angeles), Sperone Westwater (New York).

I would like to dedicate this book to my aunt, the artist Peggy Fauser, who first talked to me of the practice of painting, and my mother Maxine Benjamin who first introduced me to painting's range and depth. (Andrew Benjamin)

COVER: Stephen Ellis, *Untitled* (detail), 1995, oil and alkyd on linen, 61 × 51cm, courtesy of André Emmerich Gallery (New York). See page 64 for a complete reproduction of this painting.

PAGE 2: Jonathan Lasker, *Expressions of an Uncertain Universe*, 1994, oil on linen, 76.2 × 101.6cm, courtesy of Sperone Westwater (New York)

First published in Great Britain in 1996 by
ACADEMY EDITIONS
An imprint of

ACADEMY GROUP LTD
42 Leinster Gardens, London W2 3AN
Member of the VCH Publishing Group

ISBN: 1 85490 434 5

Distributed to the trade in the USA by
NATIONAL BOOK NETWORK, INC
4720 Boston Way, Lanham, Maryland 20706

Printed and bound in Singapore

CONTENTS

WHAT IS ABSTRACTION?

Abstract art cannot be disposed of by simple-minded evasion. Or by negation.
We can only dispose of abstract art by assimilating it, by fighting our way through it.

Clement Greenberg

Writing of abstraction within painting is already to raise two interrelated domains of activity.[1] While this will be true for writing on painting in general it has far greater extension with abstraction. The first domain pertains to the history of painting and the second to questions of interpretation; the interpretation of individual paintings as much as the method of interpretation used in that activity. Opting for a simple history would mean tracing the history of painting up until the advent of abstraction and then tracing the history of abstraction, perhaps taking into account the critical responses of pop and conceptual art, until the current generation of abstract painters. Such a history would not necessitate the use of an explanatory methodology since the linear narrative of historical development would be sufficient. Questions of interpretation, therefore, need not figure. If, on the other hand, interpretation were allowed to dominate such that all that was of significance were specific paintings, then any insistent conception of the historical would have been effaced, since the specificity of one painting within such an exclusive interpretive domain would be like any other. They would be unique and isolated. As will emerge from the following arguments what limits both these possibilities is their refusal to allow for the complexity of time.

Time, here, will be taken as present both within the setting of interpretation as well as within the work of painting. As such time can neither be assumed nor ignored. Moreover, time will come to figure centrally in any take on abstraction. What shortcomings there are in the writing of a linear history or the formulation of individual interpretations occur because of either a resistance to the question of time, or the naturalisation of time and hence its conflation with chronology. And yet here time is not being added on to abstraction. The existing critical writings on abstraction already bring a certain conception of time into play. This means that rather than merely positing a relationship between history and interpretation, the temporality proper to that relationship will have to be taken up as a question. Once this is done it will have to allow for the operation of time to occur as much in the object as in the historical site of interpretation.

What marks abstraction out is the link which already obtains between its presence in the field of interpretation and modernism. The consequence of this connection is that writing about abstraction will already be to write about the nature of modernity. Time, in this sense, will already be present. Taking a stand in relation to abstraction will involve, be it implicitly or explicitly, the articulation of a position concerning both the nature of historical time as well as the time of writing; ie the present. While the history of abstraction is not the history of modernism *per se*, it remains the case that critics as different as Meyer Schapiro and Clement Greenberg have linked abstraction to a new departure within art and thus to the modern.[2] Abstraction will have a privileged place for this very reason. Greenberg has expressed this point in a complex and nuanced formulation. While arguing that abstraction is not a 'real historical break' with 'traditional representational painting' (3. 192) he is forced to concede that the space of abstraction is irreducible to representational space. The latter precludes the enactment of self-critical painting. And yet the advent of the self-critical becomes the site of modernist painting. A break emerges therefore in terms of art's own self-conception. Significant change has occurred despite continuity. This should not be seen as merely an interpretive claim; as will be seen it is a claim announcing modernity.

In general terms what this will mean is that developments within abstraction will have to be understood as developments within modernism. And this will be the case whether those developments are the continuation of the project of abstraction or attempts – made within painting or other art forms – to plot its end. The extent to which any of these developments provides an argument for postmodernism or for another way of conceiving of movements within historical time remains to be seen. At the very least, however, linking abstraction and modernism is already to suggest that the majority of claims of a move from the modern to the postmodern do not simply involve hasty and ill-conceived arguments, more significantly they lack any sustained encounter with the question of the temporality proper to history. Fundamental to understanding abstraction therefore will be the recognition of its already present interarticulation with claims about historical time. The truth or falsity of specific claims is not central. Centrality lies in the almost primordial connection of painting and time. Denying the importance of modernism, arguing against the centrality of Greenberg, attempting to show the ideological traps that accompany (putatively or not) the formulation of modernism, for example, cannot but help take up the question of historical time since what is at issue is how the present – the modern present, the postmodern present, etc – is to be understood, and how the development of art reveals the nature of the present.

Pursuing this complex relationship – painting, time – while working within set limits will mean that in the place of the synoptic, in place of a minimal version of such an aspiration, a number of significant moments will have to be traced. Once this is done then, taken together, they can be viewed as responding to the question of abstraction by attempting to make its formulation more exact. Fundamental to this project will be the need to integrate abstraction's own development. This will necessitate attention being paid as much to stylistic concerns as to the temporality of development. An inescapable part of taking up the question of abstraction, therefore, will be repetition – abstraction's repetition. Overall, there is no attempt here to claim that these specific moments are definitive and that there are no other ways of writing on the question of abstraction. It is rather that they cohere because they maintain the effective centrality of what has been taken to be the already present relationship between painting and time that defines the inception of abstract painting.[3]

The first of these moments will be an explicit confrontation with Greenberg's general conception of modernism and the way it comes to be deployed in his paper 'Modernist Painting'. Greenberg's criticism and in particular his interpretation of abstract art sets the limits of modernism. Modernism is not just a style but a specific way of construing art's work. More than that, the way in which that work differentiates itself from earlier art does, in Greenberg's analysis, rehearse a more general self-criticism and self-evaluation that also mark the operation of literature and science in the modern period. The second moment will take up Greenberg's interpretation of Mondrian. For Greenberg, while Mondrian was an abstract painter his work was not quite abstract enough. Exploring the marginal position of Mondrian will help to reveal the implicit aesthetics at work within Greenberg's criticism. Plotting the limits of the way in which painting and time are combined in Greenberg's work will allow for the emergence of what will be described as an economy of abstraction. Even though the operation of this economy is not explicable, straightforwardly, in Greenberg's terms, it will have an affinity with that project. Indeed, the economy will be linked to Greenberg's insight that what needs to be emphasised is the internal working of the art object. The third moment therefore will involve formulating the detail of this economy.[4] The next will involve taking a slightly different tack. Here, having reopened the distinction between abstraction and representation, though now linked to the economy of abstraction, it will be possible to show how that economy is at work within Jasper Johns' *Flag* (1954). The reason for concentrating on this painting is because it has been viewed as ending the run of abstraction, and as such it has been taken as marking the point of abstraction's 'obsolescence'.[5] Finally, recent developments within abstraction will be situated in relation to the complex interconnection of time, painting and the economy of abstraction.

Greenberg, Modernism and 'Modernist Painting'

Greenberg began his reflection on the relationship between art and culture in two of his earliest papers. Written respectively in 1939 and 1940 and published in the *Partisan Review*, 'Avant-Garde and Kitsch' and 'Towards a Newer Laocoon' open a specific intellectual and political remit in which art was attributed a privileged place both in the analysis of society and in the resultant critique of society's own development. These papers set the stage not only for the subsequent development of Greenberg's career as a critic, but equally they provide the basis of some of the misunderstandings that have accompanied his writings. 'Avant-Garde and Kitsch' is a complex paper. One of the ways in which it can be read is as an investigation of the conditions under which fascism may intrude into society and its 'art' forms. Fascism operates on the level of the mass. Moreover it is with the mass or the popular, understood as undifferentiated, that determinations of class – let alone gender or race – are not able to play a mediating role. Opening up a space within the potential domination of the mass, such that it exists in contradistinction to the work of fascism means, in this sense, sustaining a site that is structured around the resistance to fascist encroachment. Indeed, Greenberg's argument with its references to Stalinism as much as to fascism is perhaps best expressed as opposing art to the totalitarian occupation of mass space. It is not difficult to see that Greenberg positions kitsch as a formative part of that space. Therefore, it is not a question of high art versus the popular but of looking for a strategy that would rescue art from the political threat of populism.

The political nature of the distinction – avant-garde, kitsch – is expressed succinctly by Greenberg in the following:

> . . . from the point of view of fascists and Stalinists, is not that they are too critical, but that they are too 'innocent', that it is too difficult to inject effective propaganda into them, that kitsch is more pliable to this end. Kitsch keeps a dictator in closer contact with the 'soul' of the people. (1. 20)

This is not to suggest that his position is unproblematic. Nonetheless it must be recognised that the attack on kitsch and the need to maintain a site where art would be able to continue are themselves part of a general problem of determining how to respond to fascism. The initial arguments concerning abstraction have this precise setting. While the nature of the link between the popular, or the mass, and fascism becomes less pronounced in his writings, Greenberg maintained a politics of art that was linked both to the continuity of art and to the formal presentation of art work. This accounts for why abstraction is linked to a conception of autonomy that does not pertain to the artist but to the operation of art's work.

Greenberg's argument, even at this stage, demands a recognition of the integrity of the work's work while linking it to the continuity of aesthetic values. These values, however, are neither transcendental nor spiritual. Rather, for Greenberg, they pertain to the integrity of art as art. Modernism for Greenberg will be the recognition and the affirmation within art's own work of there being something integral to specific artistic activities. (This recognition will have effects which are as political as they are aesthetic.) Locating the modern as historical art practice will allow him to interpret the history of painting in relation to that practice. Thus, for example, in 'Towards a Newer Laocoon' he can position Courbet as an 'avant-garde painter' because of his attempt to reduce painting to that which is immediately given by the eye and is then presented as such. Here with Courbet, for Greenberg, painting's preoccupation with its own integrity is being staged. It is, of course, only with abstraction that this process is affirmed and it is this which allows Courbet to be reinterpreted. As will be suggested in this book, the conditions of the possibility for reinterpretation are not confronted by Greenberg, and in the end, because these conditions bring another dimension of time into play, they will plot the limit of his conception of modernity.

The argumentative stance of 'Towards a Newer Laocoon' can be taken as clarifying the more general argument of his earlier paper. Here, following the opening made by Lessing in the eighteenth century, Greenberg's concern is to attempt to still the 'confusion' that is at work within the arts. His approach breaks with the tradition established by Lessing insofar as, with Greenberg, it is the historical emergence of abstract art which enacts that clarification by actualising the terms that will enable this clarification to be made. It is the productive presence of history that must be emphasised here. Part of the recognition of the force of history entails that Greenberg is neither endorsing nor opposing abstract art merely on the level of taste. After all, he asserts, he has 'offered no other explanation for the present superiority of abstract art than its historical justification'. (1. 37) However, the response to abstraction cannot take place in terms of either 'simple-minded evasion' or 'negation'. The reason is that abstraction announces a shift both in the history of art and in the sensibility engaged in the experience of art in the present.

In contradistinction to Lessing's concern with one medium making demands upon another, Greenberg's project, in this text, is to differentiate between painting and literature in order to establish the specificity of painting. What becomes central is the medium. Greenberg's own history of painting intervenes at this precise point. While it is viewed from the place of the advent of abstraction and thus amounts to a rereading – and it will be essential to return to the question of rereading – Greenberg's position is that the avant-garde has always had a concern with the medium and therefore it alone has allowed art to develop. (As will be seen a concentration on the medium is equally a concern with the operation of space within the frame.) This is not to say that all painting is avant-garde. But the corollary is that without an avant-garde, art – here painting – cannot develop. Part of what hindered painting is its reduction to the literary and thus an effacing of any engagement with the medium. This is clear from his description of painting in the 'second third of the nineteenth century'. Not only had it 'degenerated from the pictorial to the picturesque', but it functioned such that within it everything:

> . . . depends on the anecdote or the message. The painted picture
> occurs in blank, indeterminate space; it just happens to be on a square
> of canvas and inside a frame. It might just as well have been breathed
> on air or formed out of plasma. It tries to be something you imagine
> rather than see – or else a bas-relief or a statue. Everything contributes
> to the denial of the medium. (1. 29)

This indifference to both the medium and space is, for Greenberg, checked by Courbet in whose work a 'new flatness begins to appear', and then further by Manet, and the Impressionists in general, among whom there was a growing recognition that painting and the question of painting were addressed by close attention to the medium. In conjunction with this the spectator, rather than being lodged outside the work thus making the work as well as also viewing the work – a merely academic exercise – becomes the one for whom this undertaking is being carried out. In regard to this latter point what it signals is that experience – the spectator's experience of the art work – forms a fundamental part of the advent of modernity: the experiencing subject emerges as already positioned by the art work.

The next stage of Greenberg's general thesis in 'Towards a Newer Laocoon', while ostensibly involved in an attempt to show that music's own development towards 'purity' of form, and thus its overcoming of the literary, bears an important relation to a similar movement within painting, introduces three interrelated components that come to define the nature of the abstract. As will be suggested these components have a significance beyond their initial formulation. The first is the description of the effects of music as being 'essentially, of pure form'. This gives rise to 'self-sufficiency' and hence a form of interiority. The second is the importance of the sensuous, since it is the response to pure art. Thirdly, these elements are brought together insofar as abstraction becomes that which 'is almost nothing else except sensuous'. There are two points that need to be made here. Both involve time, though in different ways. The first is the connection drawn within Greenberg's own work between the sensuous and what will be termed at a later stage the 'at-onceness' of abstract art. With it the viewer is 'summoned and gathered into one point in the continuum of duration'. (4. 81) Here art is attributed the power to separate the viewer from the context of viewing. The time of viewing is linked to the object maintaining and thus containing a single temporality, a temporality that would be united in the act of sheer presentation. The object would have the singular temporality demanded by its having to be given immediately (the absence of mediation is the absence of temporal complexity). The second point that needs to be made is connected to the first; it will cause the desire for immediacy to be checked although it will not affect the necessity to maintain an insistence on the object's work and therefore on how it functions as a form of pure interiority.

The interpretive consequence arising from Greenberg's own formulations is that there is no need to interpret painting from within the framework of representation. In other words, and quite dramatically, it frees abstraction from the necessity of having to be the negation of representation.

Even though Greenberg writes of a move away from imitation, this move should not be thought of in terms of negation. It is rather the identification of another source of signification. This source will be the object's own work. For Greenberg this also resulted in the move to abstraction – in the minimal and thus negative sense – even though it can also be identified at work in ostensibly representational paintings (Courbet and Manet). This identification of another source of signification comes to be linked by Greenberg to the immediacy, or 'at-onceness', of the object and yet is not reducible to it. In arguing that sculpture and painting have a greater capacity to actualise 'purity' than is the case with poetry, this claim is presented as inherently connected to its mode of reception:

> Painting and sculpture can become more completely nothing but what they do; like functional architecture and the machine, they *look* what they *do*. The picture or statue exhausts itself in the visual sensation it produces. There is nothing to identify, connect or think about, but everything to feel. (1. 34)

The identification of the look of the object with the operation of the object can be re-expressed as the identification of being and doing. The activity of the object, therefore, cannot be divorced from its existence as an object. While this may appear to be a difficult claim, it is of central importance. Rather than demanding of the object that it presents that which is exterior to it and be positioned, and interpreted, in terms of representation, here the internal operation of the object and the way it presents itself are taken to be the locus of signification. (In the end it will be the identification of being and doing that frees the object from the hold of 'at-onceness' by opening up another economy of abstraction.)

The co-presence of being and doing is for Greenberg given as that which is singular and thus received as a singularity at one and the same time. It is the insistence on this particular conception of time that generates, and sustains, Greenberg's argument concerning flatness and the surface. Within the structure of this argument it was essential that what Greenberg describes as 'the fictive planes of depth' be overcome by a reduction to the object's two-dimensionality. Once the picture plane can be understood as moving towards a commensurability with the 'real and material plane of the surface', painting is able to attain the 'purity' that is possible for painting. It will be at this precise point in its historical existence that painting will be working as itself.

However, for Greenberg, the coextensivity of being and doing brings with it two attendant dangers. The first is the problem of decoration, while the second is the eventual redundancy of painting. At a later stage in Greenberg's writing career, particularly in papers such as 'Abstraction and Representation' and 'The Crisis of the Easel Picture', the dissolution of painting has become a real possibility, and one that inheres in the self-critical project of modernism. Greenberg links what could amount to a dissolution of painting to what is happening to the object within what he calls the 'contemporary sensibility'. Again, what is signalled here is modernism's preoccupation with experience.

Prior to tracing the development of Greenberg's own position in 'Modernist Painting' it is essential to stay with the interplay between object and time, remembering that for Greenberg the singularity of the object is coupled to the *punctum* in which it is presented. While it is linked to the threat of the destruction of easel painting Greenberg formulates this tight reciprocity between object, time and perception in terms of 'uniformity':

> This very uniformity, this dissolution of the picture into sheer texture, sheer sensation, into the accumulation of a similar unity of sensation, seems to announce something deep-seated in contemporary sensibility.
> (I. 229)

Greenberg will also refer to experience being 'given immediately through the medium'. Moreover, for Greenberg, this sensibility demands that art communicates in a way that the irreducibility of the object is maintained within the irreducibility of experience. Therefore, there exists in the formulation of this position a coextensivity between the unity of the object and the singularity of experience. It is the nature of the interplay between object and experience that has to be investigated in the light of Greenberg's 1960 paper, 'Modernist Painting'.

The article opens with the claim that modernist painting constitutes 'a historical novelty'. It ends with the claim that 'nothing could be further from the authentic art of our time than the idea of rupture'. Writing in a different context on 'Post-Painterly Abstraction', he describes it as new moment in the 'history of taste', but not a 'new episode in the evaluation of contemporary art'. (4. 197) Throughout his writings there is a reiteration of positions within historical time; painting and time are always linked. Moreover, there is the recognition that with abstraction something has occurred that has not happened before. And yet the advent of the new should not be understood as being destructive of the tradition of art. What is destructive to art is non-art taking its place; or, more precisely, non-art closing down the space in which art could continue. However, what is unique about modernist art is that it has the capacity to save art from becoming either decoration or therapy. This occurs because of the self-critical nature of modern art. Greenberg formulates what he takes modernism to be in the following way:

> The essence of modernism lies . . . in the use of the characteristic methods of a discipline to criticise the discipline itself – not in order to subvert it, but to entrench it more firmly in the area of its competence. Kant used logic to establish the limits of logic, and while he withdrew much from its old jurisdiction, logic was left in all the more secure possession of what remained to it. (4. 85)

It is because of the nature of modernism, what is called here its 'essence', that it does not establish a rupture, yet it is new and a 'novelty'. This can be said to take place because modernist art can finally establish – from within its own activity as art – that there is something specific to its practice. The way in which this is argued in the opening of the article is in terms of experience. Overall, the point being made is that the advent of self-criticism will allow for the identification of an 'experience' which is unique to art. Moreover, this cannot relate just to art in general, it must be specific to each individual art form. Indeed there must be that which is proper to each form, namely its medium of presentation. This cannot be prescribed. It emerges as the sign of modernity that each art will be able to present the 'effects exclusive to itself'. (4. 86) And it is here that 'purity' emerges; purity is inextricably linked to exclusivity.

In a long footnote to 'Modernist Painting' Greenberg draws attention to the inverted commas he places around the words 'pure' and 'purity'. Ostensibly this is to overcome the accusation that there was general prescription, on his part, for art to be pure. It could be added that part of the attempt to rid art of a spiritual or transcendental dimension and yet maintain the term 'purity' necessitated the use of these inverted commas. Either way what is meant by 'purity' reinforces the general argument about the specificity of the work. What is fundamental about the use of 'purity' is how it is linked to activity. 'Purity' means 'self-definition'. It is part of a general process that can be summed up by his claim that: 'Modernism used art to call attention to art'. (4. 86) Within painting this led inevitably to flatness. Greenberg traces a general move towards flatness: it was the move towards modernism. Flatness was fundamental because it is linked to the particularity of painting. In fact, while the argument of the earlier paper 'Towards a Newer Laocoon' was concerned to differentiate painting from literature, the project of 'Modernist Painting' was to hold painting apart from sculpture. The reason for this shift is not to dismiss the threat of the incursion of the literary, but because of the link between three-dimensionality and sculpture and their complex link to representation. It is worth noting how this position gets set up:

> To achieve autonomy, painting has had above all to divest itself of everything it might share with sculpture, and it is in the effort to do this, and not so much – I repeat – to exclude the representational or literary, that painting has made itself abstract. (4. 88)

For Greenberg 'modernist painting orientated itself to flatness' (4. 87) as part of the general process of self-definition. This is not to argue that it had its end point in flatness; instead, the key issue here is representation, and it is this which must be pursued.

Painting that is exclusively painting moves away from the realm of representation and towards the abstract. What this move is, in fact, is one away from the inscription of a dissembling three-dimensionality within the frame and towards two dimensions. Again, it is essential to note the nature of the claim in relation to representation, since what are emerging are the conditions for abstraction:

> Modernist painting in its latest phase has not abandoned the representation of recognisable objects in principle. What it has abandoned in principle is the representation of the kind of space that recognisable objects can inhabit. (4. 87)

Abstraction, thus far, is not the negation of representation. It is the form taken by painting once the concern of painting is self-definition. It is not the only form that such painting could take. The force of this description of modernist painting as in 'its latest phase' only reinforces this point. Abstraction arises once the field of representation no longer pertains. This process does not preclude the presence of 'recognisable objects'. Abstraction, thus far, is the coextensivity of picture and content; this has already been identified as the simultaneity of being and doing. Greenberg will link this to the optical. He traces this movement from Manet and the Impressionists to the contemporary. In the work of the former there was no longer an opposition between colour and drawing; there was a 'purely optical experience'. This is the link with abstraction, understood as modernist painting's 'latest phase':

> The latest abstract painting tries to fulfil the Impressionist insistence on the optical as the only sense that a completely and quintessentially pictorial art can invoke. (4. 90)

It is with the optical that it is necessary to reintroduce time. Within the strict argument advanced within 'Modernist Painting' opticality is linked necessarily to the fact that 'self-definition' is given to the viewer at one and the same time. The singularity of experience – of an optical experience – is sustained by the singularity of the work. The exclusion of the space of representation is the consequence of this interplay between doing, being and the singularity of time. And yet there is something troubling within this formulation. One way of encapsulating this set-up would be to suggest that, in fact, time does not figure at all. What is marked out as 'at-onceness' is a spatial presentation that allows for the simultaneity of its being given and received. The latter relation is the 'optical experience'. It is premised on the conflation of space and time. However, a question arises at this precise point. What would happen if a more complex conception of time were at work within the frame, providing the work with its work? Allowing for the complexity of time would not result in the denial of the optical *per se*; it is rather that the complexity of time would demand both the complexity of the object and of viewing. Prior to pursuing this point it is essential to trace Greenberg's engagement with Mondrian. Mondrian provides the test as well as the limit for what has been identified as modernist painting. Working with his interpretations of Mondrian will allow for a greater refinement of the way in which abstract painting is being presented. The key to the way ahead – both with Greenberg and away from him – is provided by that conception of abstraction which, in no longer being the negation of representation, comes to take on another form. Provisionally it has been designated as the coextensivity of being and doing. It is clear that complexity can be introduced once being is understood as involving a founding ontology of difference rather than one of simple unity. The interarticulation of ontology and time will underwrite the already present nature of a complex temporality.

Mondrian

Writing in *The Nation* in 1943 Greenberg describes the Museum of Modern Art's acquisition of Mondrian's *New York Boogie Woogie* as 'mandatory'. He also described the painting as both 'a remarkable accomplishment' and 'a failure worthy of only a great artist'. (1. 154) While this is a comment made about only one painting it nonetheless represents, reasonably accurately, Greenberg's overall estimation of Mondrian. The question is why were the paintings of Mondrian classed as failures given that they were abstract? Answering this question necessitates returning to what has already been uncovered about interiority. As has been seen, for Greenberg it is not just abstraction *per se* that pertains to painting understood as self-critical, but additionally, it is the operation of an internal spacing mechanism that allows the work to be given at one and the same time that defines the conditions for painting's self-definition. Rather than this being understood as the attribution of an intention to the work itself, it needs to be seen as an expression of the work's work. Here, what defines the work is the already identified simultaneity of giving and receiving. It is this simultaneous movement that must be retained in pursuing Greenberg's interpretation of Mondrian.

Writing of what were then Barnett Newman's new large canvases Greenberg emphasised their importance by comparing them to Mondrian's abstractions. While the setting is the possibility of maintaining easel painting, what needs to be noted are the terms in which the comparison is made:

> These paintings have an effect that makes one know immediately that he is in the presence of art. They constitute, moreover, the first kind of painting I have seen that accommodates itself stylistically to the demands of modern interior architecture for a flat clean surface of strictly parallel divisions. Mondrian aims more at external walls and the townscape that replaces the landscape whenever men collect together. Newman – paradoxically since he is less of an easel painter than Mondrian – aims at the room, at private rather than public life. (3. 104)

The reference in this passage to architecture repeats a theme that occurs throughout his writings. Greenberg links modernist painting and functional architecture on a number of significant occasions. For Greenberg, modern functionalism enacts a simultaneity of being and doing. Even though it is necessary to leave the accuracy of this interpretation of functionalism to one side, what this linkage to the architectural establishes is a compatibility between Newman's canvases and an architecture of the instant since both are assumed to be given within this simultaneity. Both are modern. Modernism is reinforced by the claim that Newman's work causes the observer to know 'immediately that he is in the presence of art'. The immediacy in question is the 'at-onceness' that has already been identified. What, then, of the contrast with Mondrian? After all, Mondrian is an abstract painter. His *œuvre* consists of a sustained number of abstract paintings. And yet questions remain: What is the quality of these abstractions? What is the nature of their abstraction?

Greenberg returns time and again to a questioning of the nature of Mondrian's abstractions. Each time it is either to link them to an earlier tradition, or to argue that they are not yet part of a tradition whose aim – the aim of the canvas's work – is flatness (flatness understood here as that state to which painting aspires in its gradual elimination of three-dimensional space). What this means in the case of Mondrian is that his paintings cannot be readily attributed the goal of self-critical art. And consequently the answer to the differing questions that touch on abstraction – the specific nature of Mondrian's abstract painting – hinges on representational space; not representation as the negation of abstraction but representation as the name for a particular determination of space.

Mondrian's work does not have the immediacy apparent with Newman. In part this is because there has only been a move from landscape to townscape. Greenberg addresses this limitation in a different article. What needs to be noted in the following passage is the way there is a move from the presence of nature *tout court*, to the reinscription of nature's own logic:

> . . . the movement that began with Cézanne eventually culminated in abstract art, which permitted the claims of the medium to over-ride those of nature almost entirely. Yet before that happened, nature did succeed in stamping itself so indelibly on modern painting that its stamp has remained even in an art as abstract as Mondrian's. What was stamped was not the appearance of nature, however, but its logic. (2. 272)

The logic that remains is the one that provides a work with the space of representation. Mondrian's work retains it, even though there is a corresponding absence of 'recognisable figures'. In other words, it is almost as though there could have been figures – representations – because the possibility of representability has not been precluded. It has been reinscribed. In fact this reinscription is a failure to differentiate adequately the project of abstraction from that of cubism. Once again what is involved here is not the intentionality of expression but the construction of the internal spacing, and thus the activity, within the frame.

Part of the general argument that Greenberg provides reinforcing this overall estimation of Mondrian – even though its detail cannot be taken up here – concerns his relation to cubism. Mondrian remained 'a cubist at heart' (3. 228) because his paintings employed a contrast of lines and blocks of colour.[6] For these present concerns it is neither the colours nor the lines that are of importance in themselves. The significant point is that their presence is the reiteration of the logic of representational space. Lines and colours work to create and hold that space within the frame. Pure interiority is traduced because the outside intrudes, in terms of its spatiality, within the work. Indeed it is a concern with spacing that forms the basis of Greenberg's own conclusion to one of his most sustained discussions of Mondrian. His position is that despite the presence of flatness the paintings retain 'dominating forms' – straight lines and blocks of colour – which means that the canvas 'still presents itself as the *scene* of forms rather than one single, indivisible piece of texture'. (3. 223) Prior to commenting on this passage (and it is the final contrast with its implicit spatiality that will be central) it is vital to introduce one more of Greenberg's judgements of Mondrian. Again, it is a judgement that contains within it the recognition of the interplay between painting and historical time.

In an important discussion of the role of the avant-garde Greenberg argues that part of its essential activity arises out of a belief that 'history is creative' and thus that art is always renewing itself. Renewal, or at least its possibility, is the sign of hope. (Mass space with its attempt to close down the space of art's renewal would suppress precisely this possibility.) Having argued this position Greenberg then goes on to place Mondrian's own artistic project in relation to it:

> Mondrian committed the unforgivable error of asserting that one mode
> of art, that of pure, abstract relations, would be absolutely superior
> to all the others in the future. (2. 16)

What lies at the basis of this criticism is the necessity – within and for art – to maintain the continuity of creation and therefore the refusal of any end point. However creation here is linked neither to the romantic hero who creates nor is it the product of art for art's sake. Creation is the province of art insofar as art is a consequence of an inescapable creativity. Despite the appearance of a tautology what is being asserted here is that art has an intrinsic modality of development. Fundamental to that development is the realisation from within art of the possibility of self-criticism and thus of self-definition. Part of that development is the copresence of innovation or experimentation, identified by Greenberg with the terms 'new' and 'novelty' and the maintenance of the domain of art. Within the ambit of Greenberg's interpretation, Mondrian is viewed as having plotted art's end by conflating finality with a style. The consequence of this last move therefore is to close down the question of art by refusing the possibility of its own continuity.

This conflation sets the scene for returning to what was identified above in terms of Mondrian's 'cubism', since abstraction – again in the negative sense – following Greenberg cannot be interpreted as an end in itself. Evidence for the predominance of the cubist mode within Mondrian's work lies within the opposition between the paintings being the 'scene of forms' rather than the production of a 'single texture'. The singularity in question involves the relationship between the work and its being experienced. The references to cubism have a twofold effect. On the one hand they indicate that even within this formulation abstraction is not the negation of representation when the latter is understood as the presence of figures. It is rather that abstraction refers to the creation of a space within the frame where art can be presented as in constant negotiation with the question of art. Mondrian's confidence in abstraction being superior to other art forms could be reinterpreted as a claim that was necessarily based on abstraction being the negation of all forms of representation. Refusing the complexity that emerges when abstraction is no longer taken as coextensive with representation's negation, would have led to the lack of any recognition of the different modalities of what appears as abstract painting. A limit will have been reached. Repositioning this claim in terms of the affirmative opens up the other effect. What returns is the question of whether or not a painting has to have a 'single texture' and therefore be given and received at one and the same time in order to be self-critical. This must be the question which arises once it is conceded that abstraction is not representation's negation and that there are several possibilities for abstraction. Responding to the latter question – to take place in the next section of this book – will open up, still further, the more general question of abstraction.

However, the possible complexity of abstraction will not mean the exclusion of opticality. What it will demand is an equally complex conception of the optical. Initially the basis of the argument for simultaneity is that with abstract painting the work is 'all there at once'. (4. 81) Opticality is defined in relation to this quality:

> . . . to apprehend this 'at-onceness' demands a freedom of mind, untramelledness of the eye that constitute 'at-onceness' in their own right. (4. 81)

Certain works, Mondrian's for example, retain a spatial setting that resists this simultaneity. But the problem is not whether this is an accurate description of Mondrian's work, but rather what guides the interpretation. Here it is essential to return to a point made above concerning singularity. While it appears to be the case that 'single texture' and 'at-onceness' are purely temporal terms (and thus it is possible to identify simultaneity with a giving and a receiving taking place at one and the same time) they are, in fact, spatial designations that have a temporal correlate. The time in question is the instant; the time in which what there is, is 'all there at once'. And yet what allows there to be a giving and a receiving taking place at this point in time is the interior of the frame containing a 'single texture'. Singularity is the presence of a singular space. This space is the often cited 'absolutely flat surface'. What is central is the interplay of the singularity of space and the singularity of time, the former being the precondition that governs the latter. In order to take up the relationship between the singular and the possibility of a more original complexity it is essential to reposition what has emerged thus far concerning Mondrian. (What arises in returning to the interplay between the singular, the complex and the optical will be presented in detail in the next section.)

Now, maintaining the link with Mondrian allows further insight into the argument that not only is abstraction not the negation of representation – Mondrian was an 'abstract' artist – but also that modernist art, and therefore self-critical art, need not be abstract as such; Mondrian was not a successful 'modernist' painter. What arises here is the problem of which sense is now being attributed to the term abstraction. The reason why this problem occurs at this stage is that by one definition Mondrian could appear to be an abstract practitioner while not being the producer of abstract paintings. Resolving the problem will necessitate recognising that two different elements are at play. The first, as has already emerged, is that abstraction has to be located within an economy that is no longer governed by representation. The second is that the identification of abstract painting must take place both in relation to this other economy, and in a retained and workful relation to the history of abstraction. (Here this relation could be through references to abstraction's own history – citation within painting – or the utilisation of other means that have emerged within a more generalised attempt to free art from the hold of representation.) Greenberg's sustained encounter with Mondrian not only underlines the importance of taking up – again – the question of abstraction, but it has also cleared the way by establishing some of the preconditions for such an undertaking to start.

An Economy of Abstraction

In 'The Crisis of the Easel Picture' (2. 221-25) Greenberg presents the threat that inhabits painting. It is a threat that works against the continuity of painting. Of the forms that this threat can take two of the most insistent are the move to an indefinite and therefore arbitrary object, and the development towards decoration. And yet what underlies the threat of a crisis is not the movement towards simple objectivity or the decorative. These are threats that are enduring within any form and for any genre, and even then they depend upon rather banal conceptions of objectivity and the decorative. There is another more implicit and yet more emphatic sense of crisis, having another point of departure. There are other threats. The position that will be argued here is that the 'crisis' is produced by the retention of that conception of opticality that depends upon what has been identified thus far as 'at-onceness'. The setting for any evaluation of opticality has already been given. It involves the recognition of the displacing of the centrality of representation and therefore the effective presence of negation for an analysis of the space of painting. In addition there needs to be the initial recognition that while 'at-onceness' is an inherently temporal term, it is equally dependent upon a spatial reduction – be it putative or not – in which the work exists such that it can be given as 'one single indivisible piece of texture'. (4. 223)

Plotting the limits of this setting needs to maintain, at the same time, the centrality of the claim that painting emerges as self-critical, engaged in the process of self-definition, once there is an engagement with its conditions of possibility. Greenberg delimits this claim with a conception of the work as that which is given within the coextensivity of being and doing. While it has already been cited, it is essential to note the next line in the passage in which Greenberg establishes this coextensivity. He continues with the claim that the 'picture or statue exhausts itself in the visual sensation it produces'. (1.34) It is this 'visual sensation' that is given and received at one and the same time; there is nothing else, nor does anything remain, the object 'exhausts itself'. In other words what is involved in this formulation is an economy of completion. Part of what determines it as complete is that what comes to be effaced is an interpretive position that could offer a response other than the claim that the particular work in question operated in terms of the immediate presentation of a 'single, indivisible piece of texture'. There could always be a description of how it fulfilled this criterion. Nonetheless the point that endures is that such a description would have to occupy a different temporal moment from the one determined by the simultaneity of giving and receiving. It would be a description after the event. The important point is not that such a possibility is resisted, but that it is not conflated with the immediacy of experience. Indeed it is essential that the possibility of such a conflation is eliminated. What this will entail is that the continuity of 'at-onceness' must be thought of as within a conception of repetition that is structured by the always-the-same; in sum what it necessitates is a repetition of the Same. Recognising the importance of the Same reinforces the point that what is involved here is the interrelationship of a spatial and temporal singularity. Moreover, there is an ineliminable reciprocal relation between them. At work here, therefore, is a series of relations in which art's work is located and defined.

Now, the question that emerges at this point is how is an engagement with this set-up to be staged? An answer to this question lies in the effective presence of repetition within the formulation of these relations. It has already been noted that for Greenberg 'at-onceness' is presented within a repetition of the Same, yet within his attempt to formulate the specific nature of modernist painting another conception of repetition had to be introduced. This conception must be allowed to emerge. As has already been indicated when Greenberg writes of the importance of Courbet and Manet there is an interpretation of their work that sees it as part of a development towards abstraction. The basis of this position is provided by the nature of the relationship between space and colour. Cézanne will also play a pivotal role. Greenberg interprets Cézanne's use of colour as designed to fit the frame. Accepting the determination of the frame is part of a movement that begins to accept the necessity of holding to the centrality of the medium. It is not the viability of these claims that needs to be investigated; rather, two questions should be addressed. The first concerns the implicit conception of the art object that is at work in them; the second relates to the position from which such claims are made. An important connection exists between these questions, and an integral part of that connection is sustained by time since what is at work here is the possibility of another temporality of repetition. Taking the relationship between the position of interpretation and the object as able to be given in the act of interpretation, as forming the site of investigation, allows for the possibility that rather than simply being given – a repetition of the Same – the object is regiven. This latter formulation indicates the presence of a different form of repetition and therefore another temporality of repetition. Since the move would be from the *given*, the Same, to the *regiven* – the copresence of sameness and difference – the temporality in question would be one allowing for an interpretive reincorporation of the object.

It is not as though these questions are simply being added on arbitrarily to an investigation of abstraction and therefore to the art work. They are indeed central. What is being asked within them can be given a precise formulation. In the first instance, how is it that Courbet, Manet, Cézanne, etc, are able to be cited as part of Greenberg's argument concerning the movement to abstraction, when their works will also have been cited as part of other, and fundamentally different, arguments concerning the development of art and their place within a more generalised art history? In the second, what is the effect on the works in question once they are interpreted in terms of a development within art – namely abstraction as the exemplary instance thus far of 'modernist painting' – that occurs after the paintings have been painted? Both of these questions point towards repetition. In each instance what is involved is a repetition of the work of artists fundamental to the tradition of painting. However, on its own this is not sufficient. What has to be addressed is the question of repetition: what type of repetition is at work?

In the first place what enables the repetition of these works has to do with the nature of the work of art. And yet art's own work cannot be divorced from repetition. They are repeated within a movement of interpretation in which a later position allows them to be reincorporated and thus given again as part of the process that is taken to lead, inexorably, to this later position. Once this position is analysed it reveals that what the work of art – by its very nature – allows for is the claim that art works enjoin a reiterative reworking. It is the reality of this position that has important consequences for this present investigation. The ineliminable presence of a site to be reworked (such that interpretation can be refigured as reworking) will not only check the assumption of a linear progression from Impressionism to abstraction, but it will have the more dramatic effect of locating art's work in its capacity for repetition to the extent that it can only be given immediately if immediacy is understood as being always already mediated. The gesture of immediacy is not denied; it is repositioned as an effect. Again, the important point is that a certain conception of complexity will intrude into what has been identified thus far as the coextensivity of being and doing.

Despite its finality there is, nonetheless, a counter to this claim which stems from Greenberg himself. Within it, in terms of art's history, is formulated a gradual evolution from one period to the next. The visual arts will have been marked by breaks and divisions within continuity. Part of the force that can be attributed to this position is that for Greenberg there is no end point or *telos* for art. And yet, despite the absence of this end point, what is maintained is the centrality of a contemporary sensibility that demands of art that it be given within an 'irreducible experience'. (2. 314) In fact the two positions – linearity of development and the centrality of experience – are brought together by Greenberg in 'Modernist Painting', as we have already seen.

> The latest abstract painting tries to fulfil the Impressionist insistence on the optical as the only sense that a completely and quintessentially pictorial art can invoke. (4. 90)

Allowing these two positions to be linked will have important consequences. What will emerge is that linear development, opticality and singularity are all interconnected such that they work to efface and therefore exclude any insistent conception of complexity. Consequently being able to argue that complexity does, in fact, intrude within one area would form the basis of being able to argue that complexity is also at work within the others.

The counter to Greenberg's general argument cannot be based on a simple contrast of positions, but on the more insistent claim that his argument already depends upon the productive presence of complexity. Indeed this is the position that has already been noted. Establishing linear developments and interpreting paintings from the position of a subsequent development within painting's history has the effect of conferring another quality on those earlier works. The important point, once again, is that the art works allow for this. In other words they are not exhausted by any one act of being given within the activity of interpretation. Even when the interpretive activity is described in terms of a simultaneity of giving and receiving the work will not just survive that moment, more significantly it will not have been completed by it. As works they are to that extent already incomplete. This claim should not be seen as a claim about the meaning of art works; it is not a semantic claim within which the inherent polysemy of art is being underlined; its force lies in the fact that it refers to the existence of the art object insofar as what is at stake is the ontology of the art work. It pertains to the object. Interpretation becomes a way within repetition of affirming the presence of the finite within the infinite.[7]

Referring to the ontology of the art work is a move that has already been undertaken by Greenberg. It is what gave modernist art its original force. His formulation of the relationship between being and doing provided a certain economy of the work, a specific description of the work's work and therefore a particular economy of abstraction. Its limit is established by what it seeks to present. Countering it does not mean developing another conception of the art work but to insist on the fact that when Greenberg reinterpreted art works, when he allowed for a reinvestment in particular works such that they come to be read as moving towards abstraction – moving towards the space of abstraction – there was the already present concession that art works have a greater complexity than that which is given in the simultaneity of giving and receiving. Furthermore, the presence of this complexity underscores the fact that the only possibility for immediacy is its occurring as a secondary effect of a more complex set-up. Immediacy occurs after the event. However the event in question is a plural event.[8] An additional point should be made here. Greenberg linked the coextensivity of being and doing to 'modernist painting', his strategy was guided by the argument that painting is only properly itself to the extent that the medium is addressed as the painting's own work. What this means, in sum, is that the question of ontology is linked to abstraction. The response being made here, to Greenberg, accepts the framework of ontology, even though the determination of the ontological will differ, however it is extended to the work of art in general. The viability of such a move in relation to Greenberg is given by the relationship, and moreover the type of relationship, that he established between, for example, Impressionism and 'modernist painting'. On a larger scale it is justified because what is at stake in general is the ontology of the art object.[9] What can no longer be maintained, however, is that the purest expression of the ontological is from within the operation of abstraction. This is not an argument against holding to the importance of the medium's self-address. Rather, it is meant on the one hand to extend that possibility to the range of painting, while on the other it allows for the particularity of abstraction to be taken up again. Developing another economy of abstraction will have to draw upon these more generalised claims recognising that they are already implicit in Greenberg's construal of the history of painting and that the generality in question works by automatically opening up the necessity for particularity.

Prior to outlining another economy of abstraction, the effect on opticality of discovering the presence of an already present complexity needs to be noted. Here only part of these effects can be presented. Opticality, at the very minimum, is a relationship between a subject and an object. For Greenberg the subject's response to 'at-onceness' involved 'freedom of mind' and 'untramelledness of the eye'. (4.81) In addition, there is the assumption that the viewer is a unified singular entity which in a single moment confronts a work that is given in its absolute simplicity. Traversing this entire site of giving is the necessity of completion and 'exhaustion'. Even though Greenberg defines opticality in relation to an economy of completion there is no reason that opticality be limited in this way. A relation between a subject and an object will still exist even if the object is redefined in terms of the ineliminable complexity that can be taken as marking the nature of the art object. In addition, this will allow for the possibility that the subject's position – the positioning of the subject – will itself be traversed by a number of irreducible determinations such that the subject comes to be at any one moment an effect of these determinations. What vanishes therefore is the possibility of there being a simple and thus undifferentiated subject as the foundation of subjectivity. This has the important consequence of allowing for both a recasting of 'mind' and a redefinition of the 'eye'. Vision (or visuality) – the work of the eye – can only emerge as a question once the relationship between the subject and the object allows for the presence of a complexity that is marked by a necessary irreducibility. The necessity emerges because the irreducibility in question is ontological in nature. Furthermore, once the object is allowed complexity any description of the experience of such an object will have to be reformulated. In the same way as the object resists the possibility of finality or completion this also relates to experience. However, this does not occur in terms of the impossibility of a final experience but rather in terms of an experience that has to hold to that possibility while accepting the necessity for a type of finality. Again, what is at work here is the location of the finite, the range of finitude, within the infinite. It will only be in relation to another economy that it will become possible to develop opticality.

What has to be taken as the initial point of departure for this other economy is tracing the consequences of the relationship between, in the first place, abstraction having been freed from the work of negation, and in the second, the necessity to hold to the presence of a complex ontology as providing a description of the art work. The temptation here is to respond by arguing that such a formulation robs art of its insistence by introducing levels of difficulty that are simply inappropriate to the study of painting. The problem with such a claim, however, is that it fails to take painting seriously. It reduces it either to an object of contemplation – a modern-day *l'art pour l'art* – or an icon, be it cultural or philosophical, in which the concentration on content and meaning robs the work of its specificity as painting. The value, and the limit, of Greenberg's undertaking is that both of these reductive moves are avoided. What occurs is another form of insistence. However, rather than just assuming that the work insists what has to be taken up is the problem of how the medium is to be understood. Such questioning involves holding to the specific nature of the work and hence having to work with the recognition that once the question of painting

– here abstraction – is posed beyond the hold of simple reductions, then the inherent difficulty of the question 'what is abstraction?' must be allowed to endure.

Allowing for the abeyance of negation has the effect of introducing into the field of painting an emphasis on space and time in which what determines one set of possibilities rather than another is what is allowed by particular space/time relations. One way in which this can be developed is in terms of a distinction that is as prevalent in the study of literature and philosophy as it is in art – the distinction is between the literal and the figural.[10] As will emerge there needs to be more than a mere transposition of terms in the development of abstraction's other economy. The temporality usually attributed to this opposition gives priority, both temporally and in terms of evaluation, to the literal. As such abstraction could be understood as the movement in figuration in which there is no longer any reference to the literal. Abstraction, therefore, would be the furthest from the literal since it no longer carries with it even a figural determination of what was assumed to be there initially; ie the prior founding literality. As is clear, abstraction, in this sense, is not only incorporated within the opposition between the literal and the figural, it also depends upon the priority of the literal. Answering the question 'what is abstraction?' will necessitate responding to the question of the literal.

If it is possible to conflate the literal with singularity in which what is taken to have a singular determination is given in a simple moment, then the literal emerges as an impossible desire whose only chance of realisation is dependent upon the recognition that the singular will always be an after-effect of that which is itself already more complex. The literal therefore is a trope; not a trope of the figural – that would do no more that simply transpose the opposition, affirming one part in the place of the other. It is rather that the literal would be the attempt to establish singularity. However, it would be an attempt that could only be successful if maintained within it was a relation to what was always other than the simple or the singular. In other words, the literal – or rather the aspiration for pure literality – would always bring with it that which turned the project into the sustained presence of an impossible desire. One of the consequences of this position is that from within Greenberg's perspective there would not be anything incompatible between an argument for the priority of the literal and abstraction (or 'modernist painting'). Abstract works would be literally what they are. In part, this position is a direct result of Greenberg having freed abstraction from the work of negation. And yet once this position is no longer determined by the Greenbergian insistence on singularity and the simple, abstraction needs to be relocated.

Henceforth the literal can be understood as the presentation in, and as, the work of painting of that which refers to the history of figures in art. To this extent it is a crystallisation within a more generalised movement of becoming. Again, this should not be thought of as the movement inside of what was outside; rather it is a crystallisation that occurs because of the very work of paint. A juxtaposition of colours and an assemblage of forms take the place of the literal since part of this set-up refers to the already present existence of 'literal' and 'figural' elements in painting. Staying at this point would be to simplify matters far too violently. Even with the literal more is involved.

Part of the literal is what could best be described as an oscillation between the resolved and the yet-to-be resolved. There are two senses in which this movement is present. The first refers to the relationship between the capacity of work to be given in one setting, and then for it to be given again. The movement from a pure giving of the Same, to a repetition of the regiven and thus of the necessarily reworked, flows from the ontological nature of the art work. The second sense in which the oscillation exists is due to the impossibility of giving the status of a representation to the presence of a literal element within the frame. There is no priority in either a temporal or an evaluative sense of that which was thought to be prior. The reason for this being the case is that it does not have the singular determination or status necessary for it to be absolutely prior and therefore to be the literal. The painted effect is not of an outside – what was outside – which subsequently gave itself to be painted and as a result was given on the inside. There is a resolution because there is the necessity to secure an identity, and yet there is also the yet-to-be-resolved because the identity in question will be one over which there is a possibility of either interpretive dispute or real conflict. There will be a resolution that, while resolved, cannot resolve absolutely. Both will obtain.

As will emerge in the discussion of Jasper Johns' *Flag*, while it is not abstract, since it does not refer to the history of abstraction, it depends upon certain abstract principles in that it maintains as central to its work the necessary impossibility of absolute identification. *Flag*'s identity is originally complex; there is no attempt within the painting's work to resolve that conflict. As will be argued in greater detail in the next section, the effective and affirmed copresence of the resolved and the yet-to-be resolved opens up the interconnection of ontology and signification. In sum, what it allows is for meaning to take on an ontological force because henceforth the work of meaning – ie signification – is located in the work of the object.

The next factor that should be introduced is the history of abstraction. Indeed, abstract painting can be identified because it has a history – there already are abstract paintings. However, the usual way of describing what is identified by the term 'abstract' is to begin with negation. Once abstraction is linked to the work of painting then a division within paintings can be discerned. While there will be paintings that seek to stage the literal there will be others that work to create their effect, and thus their work, by a continual, intentional and all-encompassing referral to the question of production. This reference, however, will not be closed. It will remain a site in which differing possibilities can be staged; to that extent it is determined by the yet-to-be-resolved. At the same time there is a resolution which is the necessity of maintaining a relation to the history of abstraction. As the particularity of works becomes central the locus of interpretation will be the nature of the individual work's own relation to abstraction's history.

There is another counter move that can still be made. This would be to argue that abstraction is prior to the literal in that abstraction seems to be the pure presence of the yet-to-be-resolved; pure becoming. The flaw in this position, however, is that not only does it misunderstand the nature of becoming, but it also has to assume that abstraction cannot be a 'literalisation'. What is different is that the site of resolution and the way in which abstract paintings work to maintain resolution will differ. It is this recognition that opens up what is central to an economy of abstraction which works with the abeyance of negation. An abstract painting holds to the generic relation whilst holding to the question of painting and the nature of the medium as central. It holds to it as an integral part of its work as a painting. The acquired freedom that is located here derives from the ways in which attention is drawn to the work of painting and then in the uses, for painting, that such a process yields. While the work is painting at work, abstraction has an inbuilt limit in that it cannot generalise about the nature of painting's work even though its very concern is that work. To that extent it comes closest to the truth about painting in that there cannot be a painting that presents the nature of painting in general. One of the important consequences of this position is that it will establish a division between 'abstract' paintings (ie non-representational paintings) which do no more than repeat certain determinations of abstraction's history, and others which hold to the twofold procedure of addressing abstraction's history while at the same time working with the question of painting. It will be this latter form of painting which will be taken up in the last section.

Jasper Johns' *Flag*

With this work there is a painting of a flag: specifically what would be identified as the flag of the United States of America.[11] Painted originally in 1954, it is a site that was to be repeated in the opening years of Johns' painting career. The flag becomes a symbol of a certain type of painting. Prior to any attempt to take up the question of what type of painting it is, there are other questions to address: What is a painting of a flag? What is it that has been painted? There are many famous presentations of the American flag. From the flag at Iojima, to the flag used by the American Museum of Natural History (the 'Gobi Flag') to symbolise the pursuit of knowledge, incorporating the flag that was at the centre of the 1989 Supreme Court judgment as to whether or not burning 'it' was a right covered under the First Amendment.[12] In each instance there is a flag; but what is the meaning of these flags? It is not as though this question is impossible to answer, it is simply that the flag does not designate an automatically singular meaning. What happens, however, when the flag is painted? Is the meaning of the painting singular? Or, as is perhaps more likely, is there a compounding of the problem since its painting entails the inscription of another level of interpretive ambivalence? What can be said of flags? Of all the American flags?

Allowing these questions to proliferate has a strategic role here. It is intended to render less obvious the role attributed to Jasper Johns' *Flag* (1954) in WJT Mitchell's polemical assessment of abstract art. It is essential to trace the role of *Flag* since it is articulated within a more general claim that abstract art is 'obsolescent'. *Flag* figures in the final proclamation of that death. In contradistinction to this position it will be argued here that *Flag* is only possible because it exploits the reality of abstraction. What is exploited is not abstract. It is rather that the founding truth of abstraction comes to be displayed – perhaps literally – within the work. While it will be essential to return to the detail of flags and *Flag*, it is, meanwhile, vital that the some of the elements of WJT Mitchell's engagement with abstraction be noted.

While the ostensible concern of his article is the relationship between abstraction and language, and more directly of painting's attempt to differentiate itself from literature, the death of abstraction is the basis of the entire argument. Abstract art is described as 'familiar', it is linked with cubism in that both were experimental though neither is now. Even though abstraction endures, that which continues, once combined with the tradition of abstract art, constitutes a 'rearguard tradition'. Given this shift from the progressive to the non-progressive (if not reactionary) it is essential, Mitchell argues, that an assessment of abstraction takes place. This position is intoned with a portentous solemnity that on its own would warrant a detailed analysis:

> If art and criticism are to continue to play an oppositional and inter-
> ventionist role in our time, passive acceptance and reproduction of
> a powerful cultural tradition like abstract art will simply not do. (214)

To write of abstraction, to engage in and with abstraction without the ensuing analysis – perhaps the acceptance of passivity – is to give up the possibility of playing 'an oppositional role'. The stakes could not be higher. Abstraction – what is named here 'abstract art' – becomes the moment that divides the modern from the post-modern and with it the politically progressive from the reactionary or conservative. What is repeated with this formulation is the already identified relationship between abstraction and historical time. 'Abstract painting' – a term whose definition needs to be left open in order to incorporate what has been argued thus far as well as Mitchell's use of the term in his paper's title – allows for a diagnosis of the present to occur. For Mitchell history has moved beyond abstract painting. This has occurred in the precise sense that its disruptive potential has been institutionalised. It survives 'as a tradition that resists any possible assault from an avant-garde'. (214)

Now, there are a number of conflations that enable his argument to be presented. The first is to conflate abstract art and abstraction with that which emerges from a rather straightforward, perhaps literal reading of Greenberg (other texts and authors are cited, Greenberg however pre-dominates). The second is the conflation of abstraction and the negation of representation. The third is the identification of kitsch with 'icons', or totems of 'mass culture'. Finally abstraction is conflated with modernist – ie self-critical – painting. This conflation has a binding reciprocity. What is not being disputed here is the plausibility of each of these moves. What they do however is reenact the now laboured, though nonetheless hardy, reading of Greenberg and abstraction. And yet there is an important absence. Despite the severity of the attack on abstraction – a mark of which would be Greenberg's re-emergence as an 'apologist' rather than as either a writer or a critic – one fundamental question has been systematically left out of consideration. The question is simply: What is abstraction? The failure to engage with this question leads to Mitchell's reading of Johns' *Flag*.

Abstraction is presented as divorced from the 'ordinary world'. Reading Greenberg literally, rather than trying to discern an implicit aesthetic, Mitchell opposes a concern with abstraction to a recognition of the importance of 'imperialism', 'kitsch', and the general range of 'social, historical realities that abstraction tries to renounce under the name of literature'. (236) Again, this is a possible interpretation. Perhaps slightly disingenuous as it elides the important point that overcoming literature did not mean effacing historical realities, imperialism, etc, what it was intending to do was raise the possibility of a self-defined activity of painting as part of a counter move to the development of fascism. And yet there is a real problem here which stems from the above conflations. If abstraction is non-representational and 'realities' are things that have to be represented, then by definition Mitchell is right. Moreover, if abstraction is 'modernist painting' and if it is limited for the above reasons, then the project of modernism is over. However once these conflations are undone another position emerges. The test case will be *Flag*.

Mitchell argues that into the modernist domain of the grid – with all that the grid entails from Greenberg to Rosalind Krauss – intrudes an element that Greenberg has tried to exclude. The flag is a 'kitsch icon'. It is linked by being itself a 'sentimental emblem' of questions of nationalism and thus the world of the popular. However, note Mitchell's language: the flag – and here it is unclear whether he means the painting of the flag here known as *Flag* (1954) or the flag – is an 'icon' (albeit a 'kitsch icon'), then an 'emblem' and finally a 'totem'.[13] (It will be essential to return to the language of the 'icon', 'emblem' and 'totem' at a later stage.) The flag – and the confusion of which flag will have to remain – is an icon of, emblematic of, and a totem for 'mass culture'. The question here is not 'what is mass culture?' but, more complexly, for whom is this flag a totem, an emblem, or an icon of mass culture? Answering this latter question would necessitate taking up the question of populism, its link to fascism and mass culture. In other words it would necessitate examining those positions that took the flag to have a singular designation. This is, of course, what used to be identified as the literal. The 'literal' is now a secondary effect. In being taken 'literally' the flag stands for a united country or a country that wishes to unite around a belief in national identity. In this sense the flag has a singular determination; it is taken to designate a single identity. However, any flag can only operate in this way if the differences constructed by such a formulation of identity are excluded. The singularity of the flag is only possible in the realm of an excluding populism – for Greenberg the domain of kitsch. This formulation has to give the flag a 'literality' that excludes its reality, namely the conflict that marks the question of identity in any nation state. And here even though these conflicts are real, the force of the argument is linked equally to a philosophical position about the nature of identity. It is only by holding to the yet-to-be-resolved nature of the flag that it is able to present the reality it designates. In other words, it is only by holding to the flag as already abstract – abstract rather than being an abstract painting – that it is then real. Abstraction, here, is the realism of the flag. What then of *Flag*, initially a work that is a painting of a flag?

Flag is of course more than mere painting since it uses material other than paint, the combination of paint and fabric work in maintaining the reality of its being a flag. It is a form of flag. Equally it is *Flag*. What cannot be forgotten with *Flag* it is that it is not completely a flag. Prior to pursuing the question of what is it not completely – ie, what is a flag? – the nature of the medium should be taken up. Here it is not a matter of returning to the detail given in the description 'encaustic, oil and collage on fabric mounted on plywood' but to a far simpler position. What is presented by this combination of materials is what allows *Flag* to be held apart, formally, from being a flag. The medium is central to the operation of *Flag*. It is only by maintaining itself as apart that it can address the problem of the flag and, to that extent, be a part of it. Mitchell's failure to distinguish between a flag and *Flag* checks his interpretation. *Flag* is not 'a sentimental emblem etc', at the very least it is a painting of a 'sentimental emblem etc'. Even then a flag is not a 'sentimental emblem etc', since it stages the problem of what it means to identify with the flag and thus for it to be a 'sentimental emblem etc'. However the question of identity and identification is presented here as a problem. Identity and identification endure as questions because *Flag* – more exactly its work – refuses the possibility of a complete identification. This refusal is the work's work. *Flag* invites identification; but the reality of the flag is that the nature of that identification is problematic in the sense that while an identification can pretend to be absolute, it is never absolute. Exclusions mark and sustain the attempt to establish a singular identification. *Flag*, because it is a flag, is a painting of precisely that complex set-up. To the extent that the complexity derives from the reality of abstraction, then *Flag* is a painting that works with what has already been described as the literal presence of abstraction, hence the reality of abstraction. Again, what happens with *Flag* is only possible because it maintains as effective, and thus as productive within its work, the presence of abstraction. Here the question of abstraction does not have anything to do with the presence of grids but with a complexity that resists absolute identification. Writing of *Flag* Fred Orton captures this complex set-up exactly:

> Flag makes a patriotic subject that contains within itself a subversion of that self. It is a subjectivity that makes itself as a disavowal existing in an avowal.[14]

The final element that has to be considered touches on the broader implications of the complexity of *Flag*. There can be little dispute concerning the presence of the work's complexity; the question that arises however derives from how its presence is to be understood. In what way is a painting complex? Answering this question will necessitate having recourse to time. What is fundamental to Johns' *Flag* is that these ascriptions obtain at the same time. Therefore the question that has to be answered is: What is the time of this *at the same time*? It is the question that will allow for the retention of opticality by providing it with a more complex temporality and spatiality than that which is given by Greenberg's 'at-onceness'.

Seeing *Flag* as purely patriotic – 'we' are all patriots united by the flag – is to have already seen the American flag as representing the American people in their totality. The synthetic whole held by the flag is thought to have been represented by *Flag*. It may be that this is what Johns was hoping to accomplish. He may have wanted *Flag* to be a purely patriotic gesture. Nonetheless, with the flag the possibility of its representing a synthetic whole is to miss the political complexity of the flag and hence of *Flag*. To see a flag, let alone *Flag*, as the intrusion of kitsch, or of the world of kitsch, into the domain of modernist art is to miss the complexity that inheres in identity. As such it works to rob *Flag* of its inherent politics, rendering it banal by viewing it as the 'icon', 'emblem', etc of mass culture. By its incorporation of abstraction *Flag* stages the problem of identity. It works by continuing the process of abstraction once abstraction is no longer conflated with abstract painting or the negation of representation.

Since the work can be described as staging the problem of identity – staging it, allowing for resolutions, but continuing to hold to the problem despite the continuity of identifications – Greenberg's linking of the optical with 'at-onceness' comes undone because there cannot be a totalising view of the work. As has already been intimated, what there is to be viewed is the interplay of the resolved and the yet-to-be-resolved. Here it is played out in terms of a flag in painting that cannot yield a sustained and unitary viewing position. The optical is retained but as partial. The optical as originally incomplete works by locating the emphatic presence of the finite within the continuing insistence of the infinite.

Abstraction's Repetition

Writing on Sam Francis and the painting *Meaningless Gesture* (1958), Jean-François Lyotard sets out some of the complex issues at work within attempts to write on art. As this passage suggests there is an analogue within painting, concerning painting's own relation to colour:

> The gesture of painting defers to the authority, the absolute, almost giddy confidence that colours have in themselves. Similarly, the fidelity of words to the immemorial potential that is in them, and to its incessant initiatives, is what makes one dream of writing. This does not prevent, but explains the fact that in the gesture of painting there is an impossibility and ban on believing in colours as there is a disgust in relying on words in the gesture of writing. In these uncertain debates, the gesture can appear to change: it tries out various turns. The point is not always to succumb to the temptation of the visible and to honour in it the obscure power of what makes it possible, but several ways are open, several types of offerings can be chanced.[15]

What is to take a chance? What would the chance effect be in painting? These questions are made more precise by being linked to an opportunity that is already there – 'several ways are open'. Once the possibility of art – Lyotard writes of 'the obscure power that makes it possible' – is no longer explained in terms of the artist's psychological make-up, then an opening exists in which it becomes possible to return to the question of production. Psychology will only ever reinscribe a humanism that will fail, necessarily, to account for art's own production. Even though it may depart from Lyotard's own intentions, a way ahead is provided by the recognition of the potential power of words and of painting; by retaining presence of the way ahead and by holding to the necessity of chance. Here, in the words that accompany a painting – Lyotard and Francis – the impossibility of finality that marks the presence of both, words and painting, opens up the question of what maintaining finitude means given this ineliminable impossibility. What is being staged here as a question is, once again, the relationship between the finite and the infinite.

This question is central to any attempt at thinking about the continuity of art. It brings with it a recognition of the art work's ontology and of the necessity for there to be work. The continuity of art must involve the recognition that the finite cannot be equated with the infinite; art's work has to do with their productive copresence. It occurs as much with interpretation – the work being able to be regiven in and as the interpretive act – as with the actual production of art. Present within that set-up is another determination, one that does not restrict chance – on the contrary it provides chance with its setting. This determination is history. Yet the history in question is not the history of the cultural historian who simply accepts given determinations and meanings. History is the recognition that each art work has to repeat the conditions of possibility for its being art. Recognising the place of history means recognising the productive centrality of repetition. The importance of modernist criticism is that it demonstrated that repetition had to be made more precise, since it had to do with the repetition of genres and types within art's history where the divisions in question were given by concentrating, at least initially, on the nature of the medium. The importance of historical thought in terms of a repetition is that, because any new art work must be a repetition, it demands that the question to be addressed concerns the nature of that repetition. Here what is involved is abstraction's repetition. What is abstraction's repetition?

Responding to this question of repetition involves a twofold move. In the first place it will mean working with the recognition that part of the repetition will comprise abstraction's own ability to engage with its history. In other words, instead of viewing each abstract painting as a unique and self-enclosed work, the work of pure interiority, there must be an allowance for the possibility that part of the work, and part of its own work as a work, will be a staged encounter with earlier determinations and thus forms of abstraction. This encounter can take a number of forms all of which involve differing relations to what has been identified thus far as the economy of abstraction.

It is clear that there are at least two different senses of abstraction at work within this formulation. In the first place there is a pregiven history of paintings; existing paintings that, taken together, provide the genre. In addition there is the sense of abstraction as linked to the relationship between the resolved and the yet-to-be-resolved. Linking these two senses of abstraction becomes possible once it is understood that what has to be repeated is the genre; to that extent the nature of resolution must maintain a relation to the history of abstract painting. At this point what has to be brought into play is the type of repetition. There has already been an allusion to the distinction between a form of repetition that involves the passivity of the conflation of abstraction and the negation of representation, and a conception that held as intrinsic to the production of painting a continual reference to production. It is this latter possibility that holds in place the question of art's work as a question. In regard to the former it would give rise to a simple repetition of that conception of abstraction that is determined by conflation, as discussed earlier. What is involved in the other is given by the fact that what it stages – and thus what is being staged – is the productive work of the economy of abstraction.

Contrasted here is a repetition of the Same and a repetition in which while there is a form of retention – hence the possibility of the reidentification of abstract art – there is the work of chance. Chance can take many forms. Here what determines and delimits the work of chance is the nature of the connection that it has to the genre of abstraction. What defines the relation is the presence of a continual questioning of the status and nature of the genre itself as a constitutive part of the work's work. The continuity of abstraction, once it is located as part of the work of this economy, will always involve a risk. Chance and risk combine in providing that continuity of abstraction which cannot be thought of in terms of a seamless continuity.

There are two possible moves that can be made at this stage. The first is to deploy what has been uncovered thus far concerning abstraction within a sustained reading of the major works within the history of abstraction. The second is to show how some of the recent developments within abstraction can be described as enacting the twofold movement of an engagement with the genre that maintains, as a fundamental part of its work, a questioning of art's own work. These are, of course, two different possibilities for repetition. The importance of the first is that it would indicate that, far from being dead or obsolescent, the reinterpretation of what could tentatively be described as the founding paintings within abstraction would not only free them from the stultifying conventions of art history, but it would also allow them to be used in arguments concerning the nature and the politics of interpretation. There is a need to reject the complacency that accepts as absolute the pregiven divisions that mark out the site of interpretation and to rework what is taken by the tradition to have already been given and therefore to be complete. What is interesting about this conception of the interpretive task is that it could not be undertaken just once. Moreover, in the attempt to undertake it, it may not occur at all. Once the work is given an ontological description that locates it in the continuity of its being given – thus regiven – for interpretation, stilling that movement, although part of the process of interpretation, cannot still the continuity of the work's own becoming. What endures is the continuity of the art work understood as the becoming-object. Attached to this continuity is the risk of interpretation. From the moment the work is taken as necessarily incomplete then the possibility of a founding criterion for judgement – the work itself – vanishes. Judgement will have become both uncertain and essential. The limits of the aspiration to present a total history and the necessity for the continuity of intervention make pursuing a systematic reinterpretation of abstraction's history inappropriate in this context. Rather than pursuing both the possibility and the inescapability of the project of reinterpretation what will be taken up here is the other site of repetition. What marks this site is the way in which abstraction's own repetition already occupies the place of reinterpretation. In this instance, however, it is located within the work as part of the work of painting.

What, then, of this other repetition? A repetition marked by the twofold movement of engagement with the genre and the affirmation of the centrality of production. A way towards this set-up is provided by time. It has already been suggested that time is at work as much in the site of interpretation as in the work of painting. Furthermore, time figured in the discussion of Greenberg in terms of the relationship between painting and historical time; and abstraction was already linked to questions concerning the nature of historical time insofar as abstraction was taken to have introduced the modern. Abstraction understood as self-critical art announces modernity. Time, however, will resist the imposition of unity; there is more than one time. The connection between abstraction and the modern still holds even with the redescription of abstraction. What continues to define the realm of abstraction is the way it holds to the question of art and therefore with the continuity of self-definition. Nonetheless, rather than there being a continuity of development, in Greenberg's own argument repetition came to play a determining role. Works were repeated. Here the time of repetition allows for an opening and thus the presence of chance, and with chance the enduring presence of risk. Interpretation is linked to the process of interpretive time – the temporality of an iterative reworking. It is precisely this conception of temporality that will have to inform the relationship between painting and historical time. To the extent that such a conception of repetition precludes the presence of either the absolutely new or the sustained presence of a repetition of the Same, it opens up the possibility of another thinking of historical time. Even though its detail cannot be pursued in this context, repositioning the art work in terms of repetition allows for the advent of this other form of thinking.

Here it is essential to emphasise the way in which time figures in the site of abstraction's repetition. Part of the importance of such an undertaking is that it will provide some of the schematic detail for an understanding of what is happening to historical time. With this particular repetition the determining effect of the genre is maintained. This means that the specific site of intervention is taken as that which has to be repeated. It precludes the utopian gesture that attempts an absolute redefinition of what is at stake. Moreover, it allows for an identification of those repetitions that simply mime or act out the genre's presence; in sum the repetition of the Same. There is another repetition here, and part of the work of this other repetition is given by chance and thus with its attendant risks. It involves a staging of the centrality of art's work as part of its work, while affirming that an essential part of the production of art – the production of this art – involves the continuity of experimentation. In this instance the importance of experimentation is that it allows for the question of the way in which art addresses its own activity as art and therefore the way the question of the object is retained to preclude the finality that would equate either a particular determination of the object, or a specific response to the question, with the object itself. What is given in this instance therefore is a particular site of painting's activity. It is not a site which comes to be represented by the work of certain painters, it is rather that this activity can be situated within that work.

While not precluding other possibilities, four interrelated forms of this activity – the work of painting – will be presented here. The first can be described as the *affirmation of the worked surface*. The second lends itself to the description of *installed paintings*. The third will involve the effective presence of *disrupted grids* and the fourth the use of what amounts to a form of *placed paint*. Thus far these descriptions are no more than labels. Each will demand that its own particularity be emphasised. What will emerge is that rather than being absolutely distinct each of these areas intersect.

Nonetheless they bring with them a sufficiently self-determined area of activity such that it is possible to treat these elements of abstraction's repetition under these different headings.[16]

Fundamental to Greenberg's conception of 'modernist painting' was the flat surface. Once the link between flatness and immediacy is severed a concern with the surface does not vanish. It is rather that the surface is refigured and consequently it becomes possible to reintroduce the surface, though now as open space without a single and unified texture. Henceforth the surface will have been freed from the necessity to be a single texture and thus will have been opened up such that not only can it bear the complexity of art's work, but it can present itself as the field of that work. One of the obvious correlates to the interplay between flatness and immediacy is that paint work brought with it the instant of its application. As a result the site of painting's activity would have been the instantaneous relationship between the painter and the canvas within which paint came to be applied immediately. Part of the attempt to maintain abstraction will therefore involve a painted recognition of the impossibility of that immediacy. And yet painting its impossibility could mean that such works simply mourned its passing, or lamented its demise. However, instead of holding to the insistent play of negativity another possibility resides in the interplay between a holding – the retention of the genre – and an opening out. This move becomes an affirmative possibility rather than the counter move of sustaining the aporetic. Here affirmation brings with it a twofold movement. Showing that immediacy denied the complexity of time arises from the work of paintings which maintain complexity and thus the work of the surface as the site of activity – the surface as having been worked – in other words critical affirmation in the place of lament. There are a number of different ways in which a complex surface can be maintained. Evident in the work of David Reed, Fabian Marcaccio, Steven Ellis[17] and Thérèse Oulton[18] are distinct attempts to maintain the centrality of the worked surface. Each attempt will have its specificity and thus its own individual effects.

The differences between Reed and Marcaccio are marked. The work of the former retains a baroque insistence within a highly worked surface. The effect of the work is the production of a smooth, almost inscribed, surface; the surface as a place of inscription. What is inscribed is of course paint's work. And here paint's work needs to be given the effect of a before and an after. In other words within the frame there is the quality of a 'here and now'; ie the movement of paint is present. The gesture of its being presented is present. Taken with that presentation is that which will already be contrasted with this presentness. The contrast takes two different forms. In its most direct sense it comprises the work of borders and edges. This is clear, for example, in the ways in which edge and border work within Reed's *#323*, *#324* and *#327*. While it would be necessary to allow the detail of each painting to emerge in a more concrete analysis, here as a general claim it can be suggested that the presence of borders and edges works to check the operation of immediacy without sacrificing the centrality of painting's presence. The traversing, yet retaining of internal border in *#323* undoes the possibility of 'at-onceness' since the addition of a division within the work, as part of its work, complicates the framed by introducing the question of a relation. Here, of course, the relation is not just between different colours but between different possibilities for paint.

Immediacy is also countered by the other sense in which there is the presence of an affirmation of presentness that incorporates what could be described as its own self-defined contrast. Here it occurs because of the way in which paint is presented. What allows for its being at the present – perhaps its initial immediacy – is the consequence of a labour and a production that while always present in any one experience of the paintings comes to be effaced in the presentation of the actual surface. Work therefore is the consequence of a certain effect, the effect of its having been. Again what would be important is tracing this effect in individual works; in general, however, with these works it is apparent in the painted effect. What presents itself as the work of paint's own application applied with a sweep is what would have been no more than a gesture. And yet the gesture of painting is no longer gestural in that it is the result of a specific form of production. It is this relation to work, or to be more precise the presentation of the complex temporality of work, that provides the point of comparison with Fabian Marcaccio.

A significant proportion of Marcaccio's recent work is characterised by a twofold movement occurring with the brush stroke. At the same time as the brush stroke appears in the frame it is present as the consequence of the process of printing and then, at times, of the subsequent activity of painting. The inscription of the moment of painting comes to be placed – printed in and then painted on – within the frame thereby defining its field of operation. *Paint Zone #5* and *Paint Zone #11* inscribe, or rather work by inscribing, the brush's activity. And yet here rather than the smooth work of continuity, the presence of painting as the brush stroke moves, its tracings, its inscribing presence within the frame, the stroke as it opens out, turns back on itself, fragments and breaks up in order to continue. What is being inscribed is the complexity of the brush stroke. Not only will this have the important effect of checking the claims of any initial immediacy of paint's application that were attributed to an earlier generation of painters, but it also opens up the question of how to think through the temporality of paint's inscription and thus the problem of determining ways in which the painting works to hold time. Part of the answer to the latter problem is that it works to hold time by spacing time. The break up of the brush stroke becomes a procedure within *Paint Zone #11* that is the consequence of the intrusion of another zone. What is given under the heading of immediacy is the impossibility of immediacy. At work here is neither negation nor a performative contradiction. The presence of impossibility has to be read back through the initial suggestion of possibility. In other words the impossibility of immediacy is not the consequence of the negation of an initial position, it is rather that in reworking the position of an initial unity that unity is shown to have been putative. Undoing it – and the site of this undoing has to be the criticism that accompanies painting – means that an innovation in the language and thus the thinking that will accompany abstraction's repetition will have become necessary. In the case of Marcaccio this will be linked to time. Not only will the temporal dimension of the complex brush need to be taken up, it will have to be set against the way in which it is presented within the frame.

The significance of time is that once it is allowed to play a determining role in criticism, its being rethought will mean that temporal complexity will intrude into other critical activities, while at the same time demanding that level of philosophical engagement in which this form of complexity is taken as insisting from the very beginning. At that precise moment the founding potential of these paintings will have been reached. Reaching it, however, will give rise to the demand for philosophy to take up possibilities which are only envisaged in art's own development but to which the project of thinking has to respond.

A worked surface is also evident in some of the paintings by Helmut Dorner. In *Grue* (1992), for example, the surface insists because of its detail. However, in later works such as '*D+F*' (1992) or *Um* (1994) something else has occurred. Operative here are installed paintings. It is not just that there are three works. It is rather that the relationship between them is an obvious, though now fundamental, part of the work's work. The nature of the relationship can be taken as operating in two directions.

Both will pertain at once. In the first place it locates within one work – and here work needs to be understood initially as that which is identified by the title – the operation of different surfaces. Each one is highly worked and yet each one brings its own fundamentally distinct activity. Secondly, what is at work involves three different objects fundamental to the operation of their work; but it is not their juxtaposition, rather the fact that they are presented as juxtaposed that is important. What this means is that both the work's interiority as well as its internal exterior relations are fundamental to the work's activity. It is this twofold necessity that has to be developed.

Opticality here involves a series of relations. However the relations are not within the work of a specific frame, nor are they given by the context in which the painting is placed. Relations in this instance are at work between the individual paintings that make up the work. While the work itself involves different surfaces what is demanded with these paintings is that their coherence has to be derived from the way in which different and, in the end, irreducible styles of painting cohere as a whole. Rather than the incorporation of different techniques within a single frame, what is at work here is the necessity of maintaining different possibilities for the painted surface within the work of a totality that is itself already divergent. The use of lacquer, for example, that provides a surface yielding a specific depth entails that rather than the surface appearing on top, as a top, it permeates the work. With a surface that works through the painting the convention of a surface's singularity gives way to a surface with depth. And yet of course from the depth comes that which fails to reach the actual surface even though it surfaces.

What has to be seen with Dorner's work therefore is neither given at one and the same time nor is there a holding back evoking a mystical or spiritual turn within art's presentation. Here there is the pure materiality of giving and yet what is presented cannot be assimilated to the moment. The splitting of the *punctum* is not just that which is necessary for the viewer, it is demanded by the internal work of surfaces and the constellation of paintings that make up the continuity and, with it, the singularity of the work.

Lydia Dona maintains the grid not as a vestige or the site of failure but as an element whose productive potential is not exhausted by its initial use. Here, then, what is retained is an absolutely specific relation to the genre of abstraction that, in its being redeployed, and thus repeated, allows for the presence of that other repetition. As will be suggested, the same will hold true for Dona's incorporation of the drip. The disrupted grid figures in both *Occupants Without Surface In The Blue Reflex Of Paradox* (1995) and

Movement–Image And The White Holes Of Multiplicity (1995). At work in these paintings is the attempt to delineate a space within abstraction that occurs via a manipulation of some of its central components. In redeploying what could be described as traditional elements they are given another quality. Rather than existing as pure elements of a process of abstraction it is as though they allow the process of abstraction to be figured within the paintings. In the first of the above paintings drips work both vertically and horizontally. They reach out backwards and forwards across the frame as well as reaching up and down within it. The drip, therefore, has left behind its dependence on immediacy and consequently the rhetoric of the distinction between the vertical and the horizontal. The drip attains the status of a figure that has come to be deployed within and as the field of painting. The same point can be made in relation to the grid. Here, rather than simply reusing its holding, dividing and ordering function, the grid comes to be repeated as figuring a use of borders and divisions that are now permeable. They hold and leak. While this indicates that such an attempt at a tight division was always going to founder it is the leaky nature of the grid that now comes to be affirmed in its being used. Again, therefore, the presence of the grid works by figuring the presence of the grid.

In *Movement–Image And The White Holes Of Multiplicity*, what the creation of the central white hole (what can be called following the work's own title a white hole) yields is an area that is encroached upon at the same time as it made. It is neither contained by the outside nor self-contained and therefore present as a pure interiority. The addition of extra lines indicating the possibility of a border is almost ironic as it only serves to heighten the fragile and thus permeable nature of the hole's divisions. It is the combination of maintained yet permeable limits and borders that is registered in the title by the pluralisation of hole. Here, of course, there is the appearance of the singular. And yet pure singularity demands a border that holds, restricts and divides. Once the borders give way – though it must always be remembered that they give way while holding – not only is there an interplay of opening and restricting but there is equally the inscription of a form of movement into the frame. Whether or not this is the movement announced in the title is not the point. What is significant is that, despite the title, the opening and closing of borders inscribes a type of activity that can be taken as delimiting the work of the frame. Movement, a process that is enacted by the reiteration of the activity of bordering and demarcating elements within the frame that no longer operate as shoring up the painting's content, would cause the aspiration of unity or the possibility of an ontology compatible with 'at-onceness' to be checked. Here it is checked in having been passed through. In other words borders are only present insofar as they are the retained – and thus necessary – site of transgression. What is transgressed, however, reveals borders and divisions to have only ever been strategic rather than absolute. Here painting is neither complacent nor utopian. Once more what is involved is a particular instance of painting's engagement with its own possibility set within the continuity of its progression.

Another significant moment within abstraction's repetition involves what was called above 'placed' paint. What this refers to is not the activity of applying paint to a canvas; this, after all, would be the minimal site of paint-ing that abstraction's repetition has undone. It is rather that it involves the recognition that the work of painting is the operation of placed paint. Rather than paint being organised to present a figure or paint being placed such that it merely eschews representation, it is possible to locate paint within a frame such that the different locations work together to create a field of paint that is no longer the simple presentation of a colour field. Something else is occurring. In Jonathan Lasker's work painting has an organisation. To this extent, it is no longer the simple application of paint, though equally it is not the chance application miming the play of immediacy.

In Lasker's *Infant Wisdom* (1989) and *Expressions of an Uncertain Universe* (1994), while each work is importantly different the question that insists with both concerns the construction of the framed. The initial temptation would be to view these works as having a syntax. Viewed in this way, that which is ordering the elements arranged within the frame could be taken out of the work and thus its content or meaning could be discussed in relation to its syntax. The difficulty with such a position is that despite its inherent formalism it makes the arrangement both too mechanistic and too arbitrary. Lasker's work is not straightforwardly formal. With his work there is neither formalism nor the absolutely arbitrary; equally there is an internal formality that brings the arbitrary with it. What has to be pursed is the possibility of this complex interrelationship.

In both paintings there is a coloured ground; the addition of lines work to create what could be taken as a landscape in which worked paint, possible figures, forms of scribble, even a possible writing, are allocated a place. And yet the problem that must be confronted concerns the nature of this ground. In, for example, *Expressions of an Uncertain Universe* (1994) how does the all yellow ground function as a ground? What has been grounded? Once these questions are allowed to endure then the initial possibility of abstract landscape begins to recede. There could only be a ground if what is presented within the frame is grounded by it. In other words there could only be a ground to the extent that the elements with the frame derive their place from being positioned in relation to the ground. Here this is not the case. The yellow ground becomes another element placed within the frame that has to be taken up in terms of its relation to the other moments of placed paint. It would be just as possible to attribute a type of grounding centrality to other components within the frame. It is in this precise sense that what is at work has an arbitrary quality. There is no overall necessity; indeed, it is possible to go further and argue that the absence of an overall necessity obtains despite an initial appearance to the contrary. And yet this set-up is not the site of pure contingency. There is another necessity. Locating that necessity involves having to work with an arbitrary set-up given by the restriction of the ground. Necessity has been relocated. It now inheres in the relationship between the elements that have been placed within the frame. Their relation is the painting's work. With any configuration – taking up one connection or series of connections rather than another – the arbitrary takes on a necessary form. It is the interplay between the arbitrary and the necessary that will cause both the nature of formalism and its relation to opticality to be recast.

To the extent that form is understood as the attempt to establish a co-extensive relation between appearance and that which determines its form, then the relationship between these two elements envisages a necessity in which their eventual identity will obviate any use of the term 'relation-ship'. With these paintings the introduction of differing internal relations strips them of the possibility of formalism while introducing the constraint of a different form of necessity. What this will entail for opticality is that instead of having to assume the coextensivity that governs a formal desire, while at the same time not being able to delight in random elements de-void of relation, looking at these paintings means having to allow the eye to work. Work, here, is not the movement of reading reinscribed in the process of viewing a painting. The temporality of reading insists upon the eye following a determined path. The construction of a narrative out of the painting's elements – the moments of placed paint – is the construc-tion of different connections and with them different possibilities. Opticality has become integrated into a structure of experience that allows the object's insistence an ineliminable necessity.

While there are evident differences in Shirley Kaneda's break up of the continuity of the frame by an allocation of different constellations of colour and design, it is nonetheless still possible to suggest that what is at work is the allocation of different areas of the activity of painting to differing locations within the frame. Here work maintains, via the use of grids, a constant allusion to the tradition of abstraction. Any initial description of either *Crude Refinement* (1995) or *The Assurance of Doubt* (1995) could start with the negative claim that what the works lack is a ground. The implausibility of such an opening is that instead of defining the work in terms of an absence it could be described as employing the systematic use of placed paint that eschews any necessity of retaining a determining ground. Within the frame there are differing areas of paint. Some work by recalling and thereby engaging with abstraction's own history, while others present a more detailed working with the possibility of painting. What marks this work is the way in which these elements combine. The placing of paint here opens up into a type of collage in which the use of grids – and in the case of *The Assurance of Doubt* the combination of grids and the large green area on the left hand side – allows for the possibility of a more complex spatial arrangement than is given either by the demand of two-dimensionality or the 'illusion' of three-dimensionality. Her work differs from Lasker's in its construction of a spatial and temporal depth that is sustained by the relation between its elements. The interpretive difficulty is being able to deploy a language appropriate to the nature of this depth. Once the surface is traversed and held up by the possibilities of different temporal moments, and therefore can no longer be accounted for in terms of its opposition to depth, surface and depth will have become interrelated. Part of Kaneda's work becomes the working out of that interrelation. Having examined these particular works – works that are to be understood under the general heading of abstraction's repetition – what emerges is a twofold movement. The first has to do with the relationship between the history of abstraction, perhaps even a more generalised history of painting, and its inscription within these works. The second is the effect that these later works have on how earlier paintings are to be interpreted, and thus the demands these works make for the language and practice of interpretation. In order to conclude it is essential to outline these two different, though related, moments.

Answering the question 'what is abstraction?', once it is freed from a dependency on either the work of negation or a naive conception of historical time, will necessitate the retention of a determining link to both the genre of abstraction and the history of painting. Holding to this link is to allow for the discontinuous continuity of painting's own development. On one level there is an unproblematic element within this set-up. The retention of a form of historical necessity is almost a commonplace. However, the difficulty emerges once the temporality of history is reintroduced as a question. Instead of assuming the continuity of development, a continuity in which terms such as 'obsolescent' have a type of currency, the necessity and the introduction of other moments within its development need to be understood in terms of differing possibilities for repetition.

Repetition unfolds here in two related ways. The first is that it provides the criteria for an interpretation of the continuity of a genre no matter how permeable the generic hold may have become. In the second place it stages the nature of the relationship between paintings within the history of painting and current activity within painting. (Clearly this lends it to a generalisation covering artistic production in its widest sense.) Greenberg's interpretation of Cézanne was a reworking – a productive and workful repetition – of Cézanne in the light of painting's own development. That Greenberg was not aware that this was at stake meant that fundamental questions concerning the possibility of this productive repetition were not posed. Nonetheless, what is essential to the way in which repetition figured is that it accounted for what was involved in the interpretation of Cézanne while at the same time it allowed for its generalisation as a process. To this extent, what emerged was a way of construing both the activity of interpretation and the object as that which gave itself – and thus as that which will continue to give itself – within the activity of interpretation.

The twofold presence of repetition will allow for an answer to the question 'what is abstraction?'. Emphasis here should be given to the word 'allow' rather than to the presence of a final and all-encompassing answer, if that answer is taken to be coextensive with a certain style or a specific generic determination. In a sense the question has already been answered by abstraction's own repetition. What has to be understood is what allows it to have been repeated. As has been indicated this necessitates recognising that the work of art – the continuity of the becoming-object – already allows for its own productive repetition. Allowing art work its incorporation into an ontology of becoming repositions the ontology of the art work within those terms which it sets for itself. Furthermore, the interplay of becoming and repetition yields a site of judgement as that which is given by the nature of the repetition. Repetition, within judgement, will always be mediated by what occasions it, namely the insistent presence of the becoming-object. Abstraction continues therefore to be given – and to have been given – within its own becoming.

Notes

1 Part of what guides this study is the necessity for a type of shorthand. (A necessity dictated by the constraints of space.) Consequently rather than trace a history of the criticism that accompanies abstraction, Greenberg is taken as the central figure. This is intended neither as an endorsement nor as an attack on his own critical positions. What is important with Greenberg is the link he established between abstract painting – and then only a certain type of abstraction – and historical time. As will be suggested, to take up Greenberg is to take up the already present interarticulation of painting and historical time. Moreover, it is a connection that, at least in its initial formulation of historical time, intends a more complex conception than that which is provided by the linear narrative of historicism. The sidelining of Rosenberg is one of the regrettable consequences of this mode of procedure. For a sustained attempt to develop Rosenberg's own aesthetics *see* F Orton, 'Action, Revolution and Painting', *Oxford Art Journal*, Vol 14, No 2, 1991.

2 See M Schapiro, *Modern Art*, George Brazillier (New York), 1994, p215. Greenberg's position will be treated in greater detail below. All references to Greenberg's writings are to the four volumes of *Clement Greenberg: The Collected Essays and Criticism*, (ed) John O'Brian, University of Chicago Press, 1988-93. The references are given in the body of the text.

3 It goes without saying that the limit being established here concerns abstract painting in the American context. It would need a separate book to try and link the projects of an ostensibly European abstract tradition to the arguments being advanced here. Part of the way in would be through Greenberg's own writings on Malevich and Kandinsky. What compounds the difficulty is that purity in that context was linked to a transcendental quality within the work or within that which guided the work. It could be argued that Greenberg placed the inverted commas around the word *purity* to try and rid it of this attribution, and in so doing to link it to the formal quality of the work. For an analysis of purity within the European abstract tradition *see* S Cheekmath, *The Rhetoric of Purity: Essentialist Theory and the Advent of Abstract Painting*, Cambridge University Press, 1991.

4 Developing the work of this economy is the attempt to further the project outlined in the special issue of the *Journal of Philosophy and the Visual Arts* No 5 on Abstraction (Academy (London), 1995). Particular attention should be paid to the following articles in that issue insofar as they played a pivotal role in the development of the position being argued here: J Rajchman's 'Another View of Abstraction'; J Lechte's 'Thinking the Reality of Abstraction'; D Moos' 'Lydia Dona: Architecture of Anxiety'; and S Allen's 'Painting and Architecture: Conditional Abstractions'.

5 This is the position advanced by WJT Mitchell in 'Ut Pictura Theoria: Abstract Painting and Language', *Picture Theory*, University of Chicago Press, 1994. It will be necessary

to return to some of the detail of this position. References will be given in the body of the text.

6 It is interesting in this regard to note that for Greenberg the first abstract painter who worked without any reference to cubism was Clifford Still. (3. 223.) What this means, of course, is that even from the beginning abstraction was neither monolithic nor all the same. These complications within abstraction are often forgotten in wholesale judgements of 'abstract painting'.

7 For a more general argument concerning the importance of affirmation in a reworking of the project of modernism, see S Melville, *Philosophy Beside Itself: On Deconstruction and Modernism*, Manchester University Press, 1986. This position is advanced in the first chapter of Melville's study which is entitled 'On Modernism'. Melville has offered one of the most philosophically acute readings of modernism to date.

8 The argument here is a development of the more general philosophical position I have presented in *The Plural Event*, Routledge (London), 1994.

9 I have tried to develop a sustained argument for a reworking of the ontology of the art object in *Object Painting*, Academy Editions (London), 1995.

10 I have taken up the consequence of redefining the nature of the relationship between the literal and the figural in Chapter 1 of *Translation and the Nature of Philosophy*, Routledge (London), 1988.

11 This interpretation of John's *Flag* is indebted to Fred Orton's remarkable work *Figuring Jasper Johns*, Reaktion Books (London), 1994. His project, while having similarities, differs over how the 'undecidability' of *Flag* is to be interpreted. For Orton it figures in the plethora of oppositions within which the work could be located and which it subverts. Orton's overall interpretation is captured in the following: 'Flag is made of two main messages or two utterances. As a work of art it embodies a set of ideas and beliefs about art and aesthetics, and as the American flag it embodies a set of ideas and beliefs and citizenship, nationalism and patriotism.' (p140) Here the two 'messages' concern art and patriotism. In the end, however, this distinction will not work precisely because what is at stake in *Flag* is painting. The two sets of 'ideas', 'beliefs' and 'values' cannot be separated because they were not singular in the first place. This is the ontology of the art work. For a more general discussion of *Flag* that situates it within the context of Johns' earlier paintings see Roberta Bernstein, *Jasper Johns' Paintings and Sculptures*, UMI Research Press, Ann Arbour, 1985, pp1-31.

12 In regard to the latter see RJ Goldstein, *Burning the Flag: The Great 1989-90 American Flag Desecration Controversy*, The Kent State University Press (Ohio), 1995.

13 Here an interesting comparison could be made with Johanna Drucker's interpretation of Flag in *Theorizing Modernism*, Columbia University Press (New York), 1994. She argues that 'Johns' *Flag* functions as both a sign and as the thing signified: it is both representation and object'. (p54) The importance of this claim is that it recognises that

there are two elements at play and therefore the important question is the nature of the relationship between them. The limit of this claim, however, is that it has to assume that the object is itself already fixed. Part of what will be argued here is that any attempt to fix the object is already a secondary effect that has to exclude a more complex and more abstract set-up.

14 Orton, *op cit*, p130.

15 Jean-François Lyotard, *Lessons of Darkness*, The Lapis Press (California), 1993. (The text is unpaginated.)

16 It is extremely difficult to finish an essay that is necessarily general in nature with a brief and truncated discussion of the work of a number of painters. The argument advanced here does not find its 'proof' in these painters. Nor is there any suggestion that all of the painters in question form a group that coheres in any direct sense. Citing a number of names and a selection of works is meant to indicate a possible direction in which an analysis of this work could proceed. And yet that is perhaps to be too cautious. There has to be a distinction between miming abstraction and the work of abstraction. Recognising that all distinctions are porous and that none is absolute does not obviate the need to establish divisions and moments of differentiation. The only possibility of being able to recognise the practice of experimentation is to take it as an adventure that assumes a certain point of departure – here the genre of abstraction – while at the same time allowing for the inscription of difference. It is, of course, an inscription that brings with it an inevitable risk. The risk of difference is the occlusion of Sameness. Moreover, it is the identification of the site of judgement and thus of the place of value. The importance of these different headings needs this setting. As headings they need to be understood as marking out possible fields of the activity of painting. The fields can always overlap and intersect. What the headings designate therefore is that which resists the possible attribution of an essential quality but nonetheless marks out differing areas of activity.

17 Ellis' *Untitled* (1995) contains a surface that is created as much by the presence of paint that has been applied directly as it is by the presence of an absence. In the latter instance it is the effect of paint's removal that becomes the central element. The consequence of this is that what is given is divided by its method of production. There are differing effects. Accounting for the nature of their difference involves having recourse to a complex temporal set-up that resists the possibility of temporal simultaneity.

18 I have discussed Oulton's work in considerable detail in 'Other Abstractions: Thérèse Oulton's *Abstract with Memories*', *Journal of Philosophy and the Visual Arts* No 5 on Abstraction (Academy (London), 1995).

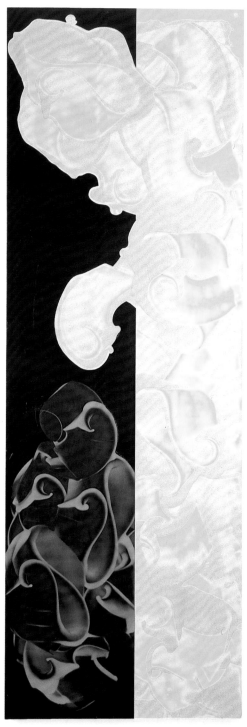

LEFT: David Reed, #323, 1990-93, oil and alkyd on canvas, 284.5 × 117cm; RIGHT: David Reed, #324, 1993, oil and acrylic on canvas, 284.5 × 96.5cm (courtesy of Galerie Rolf Ricke, photos: Anne Gold)

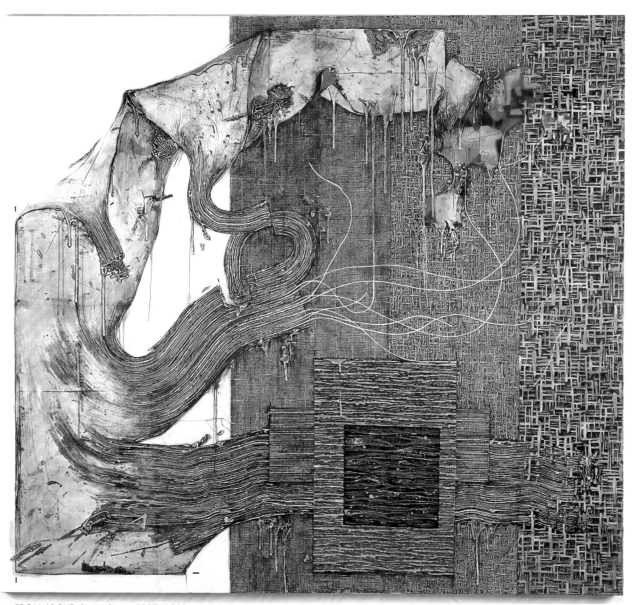

FROM ABOVE: David Reed, #327, 1993, oil and alkyd on canvas, 66 × 279.5cm (courtesy of Galerie Rolf Ricke, Cologne, photo: Anne Gold);
Fabian Marcaccio, Paint Zone #8, oil, collograph on canvas, 183 × 203cm (courtesy of Bravin Post Lee, New York)

Fabian Marcaccio, Paint-Zone #11, 1994-95, oil, collograph on canvas, 162.5 × 152.5cm (courtesy of Bravin Post Lee, New York)

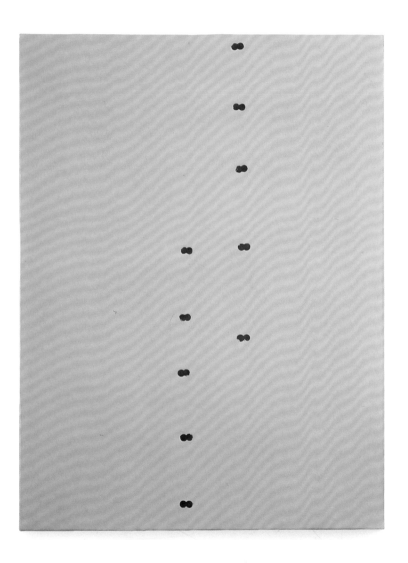

Helmut Dorner, D+F, 1992, three parts, from left to right: Varnish/Wood, 130 × 97 × 9cm; Oil/Wood, 48 × 55 × 7cm; Varnish/Plexiglass, 62 × 50 × 8.5cm
(courtesy of Galerie Bärbel Grässlin)

Lydia Dona, Occupants Without Surface In The Blue Reflex Of Paradox, *1995, oil, acrylic and sign paint on canvas, 213 × 162.5cm*
(courtesy of LA Louver, Los Angeles)

Lydia Dona, Movement-Image And The White Holes Of Multiplicity, *oil, acrylic and sign paint on canvas, 213 × 162.5cm*
(courtesy of LA Louver, Los Angeles)

Jonathan Lasker, Infant Wisdom, 1989, oil on linen, 190.5 × 2254cm (courtesy of Sperone Westwater, New York)

Jonathan Lasker, Natural Order, 1993, oil on linen, 296 × 243.8cm (courtesy of Sperone Westwater, New York)

Shirley Kaneda, The Assurance of Doubt, *1995, oil and acrylic on linen, 190 × 157.5cm (courtesy of Jack Shainman Gallery, New York)*

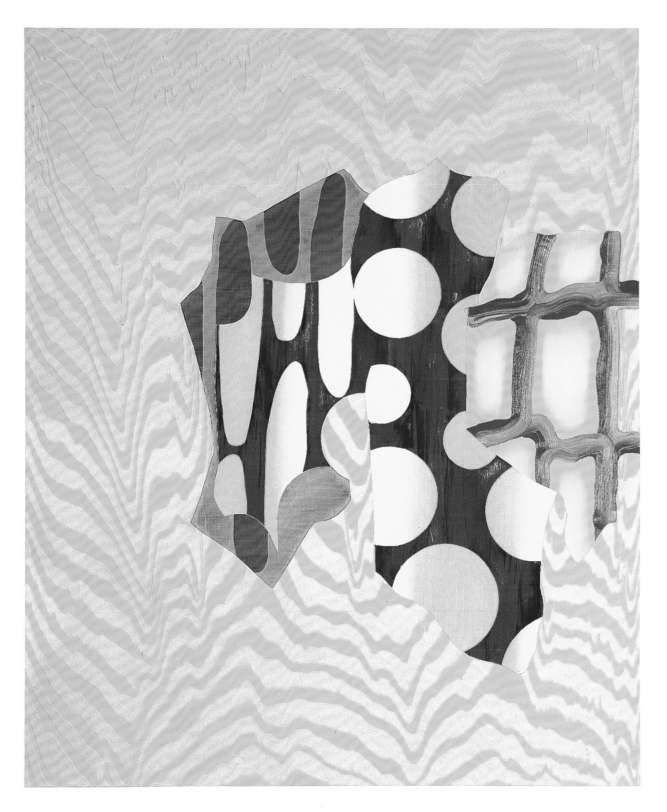

Shirley Kaneda, The Sensual Duplicity, *1995, oil on linen, 91.44 x 76.2cm (courtesy of Feigen Inc, Chicago)*

FURTHER READING

There are a great many books written on the history of abstract art. In addition there are volumes containing papers and documents by and on artists working within the abstract tradition. Three volumes that can be usefully consulted for history and documents are:

S Guilbaut (ed), *Reconstructing Modernism: Art in New York, Paris and Montreal 1945-1964*, MIT Press (Cambridge, USA), 1990

D Schapiro and C Schapiro (eds), *Abstract Expressionism: A Critical Record*, Cambridge University Press (Cambridge, UK), 1990

Paul Wood et al, *Modernism in Dispute: Art Since the Forties*, Yale University Press (New Haven, USA), 1993

While there are many theoretical works that deal with abstraction either wholly or in part, perhaps the most significant are the following:

Y-A Bois, *Painting as Model*, MIT Press (Cambridge, USA), 1990

H Damisch, *Fenêtre jaune cadmium, ou les dessous de la peinture*, Editions du Seuil (Paris, France), 1984

J Drucker, *Theorizing Modernism: Visual Art and the Critical Tradition*, Columbia University Press (New York, USA), 1994

R Krauss, *The Originality of the Avant-Garde and Other Modernist Myths*, MIT Press (Cambridge, USA), 1986

R Krauss, *The Optical Unconscious*, MIT Press (Cambridge, USA), 1993

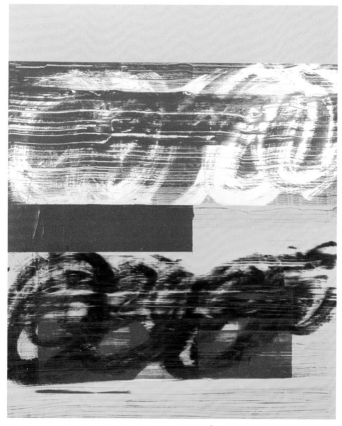

ABOVE: Stephen Ellis, Untitled, 1995, oil and alkyd on linen, 61 × 51cm (courtesy of André Emmerich Gallery, New York)